DEAR SCENIC DRIVER:

When it comes to our landscape, Utahns burst with pride. All of us, whatever our convictions or beliefs, are passionate about Utah's outdoors.

We have 84,900 square miles of land in Utah, and for now anyway, not too many people per square foot. In the north, where the mountains, the water, and most of the people are, it's a high desert and alpine environment. The mysterious Great Salt Lake beats a steady slap at the western borders of our major cities, and the Rockies flank our east, cradling snow-fed mountain lakes that the hottest summer sun can't warm.

About halfway down the state, the Colorado Plateau takes over, and the mountains slowly narrow into ribbons and hoodoos of colored rock. The far south reaches are crowded with geologic twists of red and gold rock so wondrous and fragile they have been awarded with protection of five national parks and a 1.9 million acre national monument.

We've wandered all over our state for dozens of years, and this book is meant to show you our favorite pathways. Some teem with local history, some lead to recreation sites, some get close-up to wildlife, all are scenic.

Even if this time you're in a hurry (you can navigate our entire state on exquisite, seamless freeways in a day) come back next time and take the long way home. Utah's 26 byways and 58 backways are waiting. Pack some water, snacks and a map, put on a seatbelt – and have a wonderful trip.

Sincerely,

UTAH SCENIC BYWAY COMMITTEE

Utah! SCENIC Byways and Backways

A DOZEN YEARS AGO, A RURAL TOWN IN UTAH CONDUCTED A SURVEY. THE GOAL WAS TO ENCOURAGE

LOCAL TOURISM — AND ONE OF THE SURVEY ANSWERS WAS A SURPRISE: VISITORS LOVE TO DRIVE. SPECIFICALLY,

VISITORS WANT THEIR DRIVE TO BE SCENIC AND THEY WANT THEIR EXPERIENCE TO BE

UNIQUE. WHAT NOW SEEMS OBVIOUS WAS THEN A NEW CONCEPT — "WHY NOT SHOW

VISITORS THE SCENIC DRIVES THAT LEAD TO UTAH'S RURAL TOWNS? AND ALONG THE WAY,

WHY NOT GIVE THEM SOMETHING AUTHENTIC, SOMETHING UNIQUE, TO DO AND SEE?" IN THE YEARS SINCE,

"HERITAGE TOURISM" "CULTURAL TOURISM" "CREATING A SENSE OF PLACE" AND "WESTERN EXPERIENCE" HAVE ALL

BECOME POPULAR VACATION THEMES. BUT THEY ALL BEGAN WITH THE CONCEPT OF BYWAYS AND BACKWAYS,

SHOWING VISITORS THE WAY — LITERALLY — TO OUR HIDDEN TREASURES. THIS BOOK

IS THE PRODUCT OF YEARS OF HONING AND CONDENSING AND UPLIFTING OUR MASSIVE

SYSTEM OF SCENIC ROADS. IN A STATE WHERE MOST OF OUR ROADS ARE TRULY SCENIC,

WE PRESENT A SYSTEM OF TWENTY-SIX BYWAYS AND FIFTY-EIGHT BACKWAYS — THE VERY

BEST DRIVES THAT UTAH HAS TO OFFER. THE ROADS HAVE "MADE THE GRADE" NOT ONLY BECAUSE OF THEIR

SCENERY, BUT ALSO THEIR ADDITIONAL ATTRIBUTES — THE HISTORY, RECREATION, ARCHEOLOGY AND CULTURE THAT

IS PAIRED WITH THE BEAUTY OF THE ROADS. ADDITIONALLY, AND PERHAPS MOST IMPORTANTLY, EACH OF THE BYWAYS

HAS ITS OWN GROUP OF LOCAL CHAMPIONS — PEOPLE WHO LIVE AND WORK NEAR THE

ROAD AND CARE ABOUT IT ENOUGH TO PLEDGE TO PRESERVE ITS UNIQUE QUALITIES.

THIS BOOK IS DIVIDED INTO TWO PARTS — FIRST A DESCRIPTION OF OUR BYWAYS: PAVED

ROADS THAT ARE GENERALLY SAFE, YEAR-ROUND, FOR A PASSENGER CAR. SECONDLY OUR BACKWAYS: ROADS THAT

OFTEN REQUIRE A FOUR-WHEEL DRIVE, AND WHERE IT'S BEST TO ASK LOCALLY FOR WEATHER AND ROAD CONDITIONS.

Utah!
SCENIC Byways

I N THE NEXT 50 PAGES, each of Utah's designated **Byways** is detailed with route descriptions, maps and photographs. These roads are known for their outstanding beauty as well as the experiences they offer visitors in recreation, heritage, and wildlife watching.

Most Byways are described traveling from south to north or from west to east. In actuality, with the exception of a few roads, the **Scenic Byways** may be enjoyed by traveling in either direction.

Scenic Byways are major roads that are regularly traveled. Some welcome visitors with information centers, interpretive brochures and signage. Some offer simply a stretch of undisturbed views. All are marked with colorful highway signs. For your reference, the **Byways** are also indicated with dotted lines on the official **Utah highway map**.

Some **Utah! Scenic Byways** have also been designated as **National Scenic Byways** by the Federal Highway Administration. For more information about **Americas Byways** visit www.byways.org.

Actual travel speeds are generally less than the typical 55 mile-per-hour speed limit. As with all motor vehicle travel, personal discretion is the key to a safe driving experience. Please drive carefully, and enjoy Utah's beautiful roads.

Left Photo: Fishlake Scenic Byway, No. 16 (pg 38) — Frank Jensen

Top Lt Photo: Mirror Lake Scenic Byway, No. 6 (pg 18) — Frank Jensen

Top Rt Photo: Natural Bridges NM, Bicentennial Scenic Byway, No. 14 (pg 34) — Frank Jensen

Bottom Rt Photo: Hwy 12 Scenic Byway, No. 18 (pg 42) — Tom Till

Utah!
SCENIC Byways

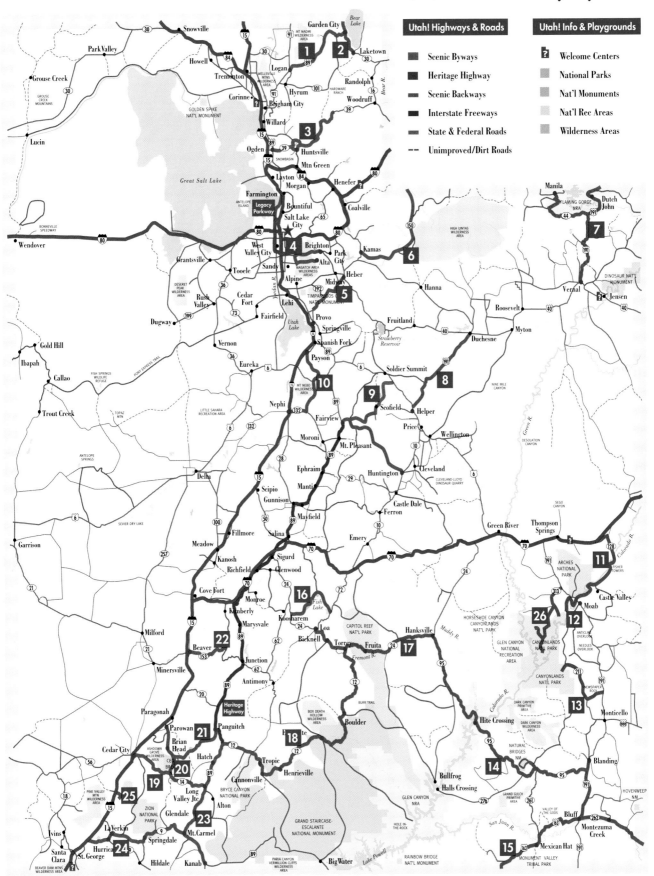

Utah! SCENIC Byways

Utah! Highways & Roads

- **Scenic Byways**
- **Heritage Highway**
- **Scenic Backways**
- **Interstate Freeways**
- **State & Federal Roads**
- **Unimproved/Dirt Roads**

Utah! Info & Playgrounds

- **?** Welcome Centers
- National Parks
- Nat'l Monuments
- Nat'l Rec Areas
- Wilderness Areas

LOGAN CANYON
Scenic Byway

US-89 from Logan to the
Utah/Idaho border

How do I get there? The Byway begins four miles east of Logan and continues northeast through the spectacular Wasatch-Cache National Forest to turquoise-hued Bear Lake, which spans the Utah/Idaho border.

What can I see and do? A great starting place is the Logan Ranger District Office, located four miles east of downtown Logan at the entrance to the Canyon. At this rest stop and visitor information center, interpretive signs and displays tell the history of the Byway and surrounding Cache Valley. See the

levels of ancient Lake Bonneville. Learn about the Shoshone Indians, the mountain men and the Mormon pioneers who once roamed and settled these mountains. Pickup a free brochure entitled: "A Scenic Guide to Logan Canyon: 32 Sites and Stops." Set your odometer to zero and follow the guide as it points out interpretive displays, hiking trails, biking trails, picnic areas and favorite stops. Each stop details the history of the people who forged this road as well as the geographic forces that created this canyon.

You will see spectacular scenery: forested canopies, limestone outcroppings, winding rivers and fields of wildflowers. There are 500 million years of geologic history in the rock formations, limestone cliffs, rugged rocks, spectacular overlooks and falls that surround you.

Scenic Logan Canyon has a full range of recreational activities. The Logan River is popular with fly fishermen, and the three dams in the Canyon are filled with mountain trout. The visitor information centers have detailed guides with information on the many excellent hiking and biking trails accessible from the road. Along many of the hiking trails you can find fossils from the prehistoric days when the shores of Lake Bonneville crept up the canyon walls. Campgrounds and picnic areas are located all along the route.

A variety of colorful vegetation is found all through the Canyon. Each autumn, the fall color displays are unparalleled. In winter, Logan Canyon becomes a mecca for snowmobilers, with access to over 350 miles of groomed trails. Downhill skiing is available at the Beaver Mountain Ski Resort. Winter is a great time for spotting moose, deer and elk.

Elevations in the Canyon range from 4,700 feet at the mouth to nearly 7,800 feet at the summit. A strongly recommended seven–mile side tour leads to Tony Grove Lake, a spectacular glacial lake.

What is the one-way, no-stops drive time?
The 41-mile drive requires approximately one hour.

For more information: Call the Cache Valley Tourism office at 435-752-2161 or 800-882-4422.

Large Photo: Autumn splendor comes to Logan Canyon – Frank Jensen
Inset Photo: The limestone outcroppings of Logan Canyon – Frank Jensen

BEAR LAKE
Scenic Byway

SR-30 from Garden City
south to Laketown

How do I get there? You can access the Byway at either end – traveling from the west through Logan Canyon and US-89, turn south onto SR-30 at the town of Garden City; traveling from the east, turn west onto SR-30 at Sage Creek Junction (the junction of SR-16 and SR-30). This Byway travels the western shore of Bear Lake.

What can I see and do? Both Garden City and Laketown are small agricultural towns that have grown to accommodate the crowds that descend on Bear Lake in the warm months. Garden City has several drive-ins famous for raspberry shakes – the local specialty – and a visitor center. Laketown has a pioneer-era mercantile that is a fun stop for snacks and soda.

The Byway travels along the shoreline of turquoise-colored Bear Lake. Straddling the Utah/Idaho border, the lake was named by early fur trappers who found the surrounding valley full of black bears, beaver and other animals. Bear Lake also served as a summer meeting ground for Native American tribes, mostly Shoshone and Bannock. In the early 1800s, hardy mountainmen held their annual rendezvous' here. These often-raucous events were attended by the likes of Jim Bridger and Jedediah Smith. Mormon pioneer settlement to the area occurred in the early 1860s, led by Charles C. Rich.

The color of the lake is a wonder to behold. The turquoise blue is due to light reflecting off the limestone particles suspended in the water. Bear Lake is 20 miles long and eight miles wide and has a reported depth of 208 feet. Many stories are told about the elusive "Bear Lake Monster" that roams the depths.

The Lake is a popular watersport haven for boating, sailing, jet skiing, fishing and swimming. Bear Lake State Park is located along the Byway, with camping, picnicking, boat rental and launching facilities available. January and early February bring hundreds of people who brave the cold to catch the spawning Bonneville Cisco. The area is also a popular snowmobile and cross-country skiing retreat for winter visitors.

Located alongside the Byway are two paths worthy of a visit: the Bear Lake Trail is a biking/walking trail leading from Bear Lake State Park Marina to Ideal Beach; and a raised walkway from Garden City Park, over a marsh to the Lake, has interpretive signs describing local flora and fauna.

What is the one-way, no stops drive time?
The Byway is approximately 15 miles long and travel time is about 25 minutes.

For more information:
Call 800-448-BEAR.

Large Photo: The color of Bear Lake is a wonder to behold – Scott Smith

Inset Photo: Bear Lake is a popular watersport haven – Frank Jensen

OGDEN RIVER
Scenic Byway

SR-39 from Ogden to the eastern Wasatch-Cache National Forest boundary, including the road around Pineview Reservoir

How do I get there? The Byway begins in the city of Ogden. Find 12th Street, and head east until you come to the mouth of Ogden Canyon. The road travels up Ogden Canyon, around Pineview Reservoir, passes Monte Cristo Peak, and ends at the Forest Service boundary, near the town of Woodruff.

What can I see and do? The Byway can be roughly divided into three parts – Ogden Canyon, Pineview Reservoir, and the Monte Cristo Road. All provide separate aesthetics and all are stunning. The Ogden River is responsible for all three – carving the narrow canyon, providing water for its modern reservoirs, and creating Monte's alpine valleys.

Once you enter the Canyon, the road quickly narrows and its cliff walls are steep, rugged and wildly beautiful, with layers of limestone and shale streaked with cream, pink and red. You'll find not only alpine beauty here, but excellent fishing and hiking. Popular trailheads include Coldwater Canyon and Wheeler Creek Canyon. A favorite family hike is Indian Trail, with five miles of winding forest trail tucked neatly into the mountainside.

The scenic Pineview Reservoir and dam are six miles east, perched at the top of the canyon and greeting visitors like a big surprise. Water recreation is popular here year-round, and the Wasatch-Cache National Forest has supplied boat ramps and camping and picnicking facilities. The Byway loops around the entire Reservoir. A worthwhile stop for bird watchers is the adjacent Ogden Bay Waterfowl Management Area's North Arm Viewing Site, with its own pedestrian nature trail.

Off-shoot roads lead to Snowbasin (site of the alpine skiing speed competitions of the 2002 Olympic Winter Games) and Powder Mountain ski resorts.

Back on the main road, keep traveling to the town of Huntsville. Once past town the road begins a steep ascent, traveling South Fork Canyon and following the south fork of the Ogden River through heavily wooded landscapes. There are several lovely camp-sites here. Immediately past South Fork Canyon, a junction leads to the fishing haven of Causey Reservoir.

As you continue on SR-39, vista after scenic vista will spread before you. This is one of the stellar views in the West. As the Byway nears Monte Cristo summit, you can glimpse views of 9,148-foot Monte Cristo Peak through stands of spruce and Douglas fir.

Fall colors along the entire road are spectacular. Because of snow conditions, portions of the route are closed in the winter. Dates of closure depend on snowfall.

What is the one way, no stops drive time? This 44-mile Byway requires approximately one hour and 15 minutes.

For more information: Call Ogden Visitor Information at 801-627-8288 or the Ogden Ranger District at 801-625-5306.

Large Photo: Pineview Reservoir is perched at the top of Ogden Canyon – Steven Greenwood

Top Photo: Water recreation is popular at Pineview – Frank Jensen

GREAT
SALT
LAKE

91
Brigham City

MONTE
CRISTO
PEAK

39
Woodruff

POWDER
MTN

PINEVIEW
RESERVOIR

15

39

Ogden

39
Huntsville

SNOWBASIN

84
Mountain Green

BIG & LITTLE COTTONWOOD CANYONS
Scenic Byway

SR-190 from the mouth of Big Cottonwood Canyon to Brighton, SR-210 from the mouth of Little Cottonwood Canyon to Alta

How do I get there? To reach both Big and Little Cottonwood Canyons take I-215 to the 6200 South/Canyons exit (about 25 miles southeast of Salt Lake City). Follow the signs to SR-190 for Big Cottonwood Canyon, home to Solitude and Brighton Resorts. Follow the signs to SR-210 for Little Cottonwood Canyon, home to Alta and Snowbird Resorts.

What is there to see and do? Known locally as "Big" and "Little," the Canyons are located side by side, but dissect and plunge headlong into separate crevice formations of the Wasatch-Cache National Forest. The Wasatch Mountains are the westernmost wall of the Rockies, and both routes ascend to about 12,000 feet.

From the main road Big Cottonwood Canyon narrows almost immediately to dramatic alpine scenery. Its 15 miles provide excellent hiking, picnicking, rock climbing, camping and fishing. One of the most popular hiking trails begins at Mill B South Fork and leads to Lakes Blanche, Florence and Lillian. The trail is 3.1 miles long and is considered strenuous. An easier hiking area begins at Brighton Resort's large parking lot. Several trails lead to various lakes, including Twin Lakes, Lake Mary, Lake Martha, Lake Catherine and Dog Lake.

The major ski and summer resorts of Solitude and Brighton are located near the top of Big Cottonwood Canyon. Both have full-service, year-round facilities. In winter, both resorts have plenty of steep terrain for expert skiers, but are beloved by families because of their kinder, gentler beginner hills. A quarter-mile below Brighton is Solitude Nordic Center, with a half-mile of flat, groomed track, as well as steep, offshoot trails that are more challenging.

Large Photo: Silver Lake sunrise, Brighton, Big Cottonwood Canyon — Tom Till
Inset Photo: Albion Basin wildflowers, Alta, Little Cottonwood Canyon — Bill Crnkovich

Big Cottonwood Canyon is a protected watershed area and no dogs are permitted. Wilderness areas are located to the north and south.

Little Cottonwood Canyon is so named because its length and width are "littler" than its big neighbor to the north, however it is an equally glorious natural playground. If you're a first-timer, you may well be awestruck by the sheer ruggedness and beauty of the glacially-carved corridor. At the mouth of the Canyon is the site where Mormon pioneers quarried the massive granite blocks used to construct the Salt Lake Temple, and more recently The LDS Conference Center.

Little Cottonwood is home to two of Utah's ski and summer resorts. At world-class Snowbird, Utah's only aerial tramway carries visitors to the roof of the Rockies for a panoramic view from 11,000-foot Hidden Peak – a ski destination in winter, and a hiking destination in summer. One mile further up the main road is Alta. Notorious for shootings in its 26 saloons during the mining days of the 1860s and 70s, Alta's boom went bust – but then livened up again in 1938 as the site of Utah's first ski resort. There are several excellent, full-service, year-round lodges here. The Albion Basin that encompasses Alta is famous for wildflowers and is one of the most photographed areas in northern Utah.

Wilderness areas are located on both sides of Little Cottonwood. Recreational activities on the route include rock climbing, camping, picnicking, mountain biking and hiking (and eating at great restaurants!). Little Cottonwood is part of Salt Lake City's watershed area and no dogs are allowed.

What is the one-way, no-stops drive time?
Both canyons are one-way, in-and-out drives. Big Cottonwood is 15 miles long, Little Cottonwood is seven miles long. Travel time from Salt Lake City to the top of each separate Canyon is about 45 minutes.

For more information: Call Wasatch-Cache National Forest information at 801-524-3900.

PROVO CANYON
Scenic Byway

US-189 from its junction with SR-52 (just north of Provo) to Heber City

How do I get there? Traveling on I-15, exit at Orem #275 and head east on 8th North (SR-52) until you come to US-189 and Provo Canyon. If you begin your trip in Heber City, head south and follow the signs to US-189.

What is there to see and do? The Byway winds through wide, wonderful Provo Canyon, past Bridal Veil Falls and Deer Creek Reservoir, and on to the scenic Heber Valley.

If you leave from Provo or Orem, the road parallels the Provo River, one of the world's premiere fly-fishing streams. The dynamic forces of a past era are revealed

in the canyon's gnarled rock walls and jagged rock formations, lush with forest vegetation. Just a few miles up Provo Canyon is the trail-head for Squaw Peak Trail, which offers dramatic and spectacular views of Utah Valley. Bridal Veil Falls, a double-cataract waterfall, can be seen from the road.

It takes its name from the intricate, lacy pattern the water makes as it flows over rock boulders.

A worthwhile side trip is the Alpine Scenic Loop (SR-92), a narrow, windy road famous for fall color drives. It leads past Robert Redford's year-round Sundance Resort, famous for family skiing in winter and outdoor theater in summer; the Uinta National Forest; and Timpanogos Cave National Monument.

Large Photo: Bridal Veil Falls in Provo Canyon — Tom Till
Inset Photo: Mount Timpanogos peaks through the clouds — Frank Jensen
Right Top Photo: Winter reflections of Timpanogos, Deer Creek Reservoir — Mel Lewis

The Cave is a fee area, requires tickets, and has a steep climb to its entrance – but its colorful caverns and mysterious, beating "heart" are a destination for many vacationers.

Back on the Byway, at the top of Provo Canyon, Deer Creek Reservoir State Park has sailing, boating, fishing and windsurfing.

The Byway's end is Heber Valley, home of the Heber Valley Railroad. This historic train has a schedule of tours through Heber Valley and Provo Canyon during most of the year. Nearby, on SR-113 is the quaint town of Midway, and further on in Soldier Hollow, part of Wasatch Mountain State Park, is a network of excellent cross-country trails, built for the 2002 Olympic Winter Games' biathlon competitions. It is available to the public before and after the Games.

What is the one-way, no-stops drive time?

The Provo Canyon Scenic Byway is 28 miles long and travel time is about 45 minutes.

For more information: Call Mountainland Travel Region at 801-229-3800.

MIRROR LAKE
Scenic Byway

SR-150 from Kamas
to the Utah/Wyoming Border

How do I get there? Heading east and north from Kamas through the Wasatch-Cache National Forest to the Wyoming border and beyond... Once across the border, SR-150 continues to the town of Evanston, and is a designated Wyoming Scenic Byway.

What is there to see and do? The Mirror Lake road is one of the most popular mountain routes in Utah and Wyoming. From Kamas, the Byway winds through farm and ranch lands, and rises to heavily forested, mountain terrain, accented by meadows and rugged mountain peaks.

In addition to scenic viewpoints, picnic areas and campgrounds, the Byway provides access to many of the 400 lakes found throughout the Uinta Range. The U-shaped valleys were carved by ancient

glaciers during the last ice age. Much of the journey parallels the Provo River. At Upper Provo River Falls, 24 miles from Kamas, you can view terraced cascades from walkways near the road.

The Byway climbs to an elevation of 10,687 feet at Bald Mountain Pass before descending past Mirror Lake, which is a fee area, then to Bear River Ranger Station and its "Historical Tie Hack Cabin." From here the route parallels the Bear River (the longest river in the western hemisphere which does not flow into an ocean) and passes on to Evanston.

Recreation activities along the Byway include camping, fishing, cross-country skiing and hiking. The area is also used as access to the High Uinta Wilderness. Heavy snowfall in winter closes the Byway to car traffic, but remains open for snowmobiles.

What is the one-way, no stops drive time?
The Utah portion of the Byway is 55 miles long, with another 23 miles to Evanston. Total travel time is about two hours.

For more information: Call Mountainland Travel Region at 801-229-3800 or the Kamas Region District Office at 435-783-4338.

Large Photo: View of Hayden Peak from Mirror Lake Scenic Byway – Steve Greenwood
Inset Photo: Christmas Meadows – Frank Jensen
Bottom Right Photo: Early winter dusting at North Fork – Steve Greenwood

WYOMING

TO
EVANSTON

80

Coalville

Wanship

80

40

JORDANELLE
RESERVOIR

Kamas

189

Heber

150

MIRROR
LAKE

HIGH
UINTAS
WILDERNESS

Upper Provo River

FLAMING GORGE-UINTAS
National Scenic Byway

US-191 north from Vernal
to the Utah/Wyoming border;
and from the junction of
US 191/44 to Manila

How do I get there? Access the Byway from any of its three entrances: from Vernal's Main Street, head northeast on US-191; from Manila head south on SR-44; from Dutch John head south on US-191.

What is there to see and do? The stunning Byway travels through the Ashley National Forest, over the eastern flank of the Uinta Mountains, and skirts the Flaming Gorge National Recreation Area. It is designated a National Scenic Byway by the Federal Highway Administration, and a National Forest Scenic Byway by the U.S. Forest Service.

The Byway's signature theme is "Wildlife Through the Ages," and interpretive signs and pull-off kiosks tie together the presence of abundant wildlife, world-renowned fossilized dinosaur remains, and spectacular scenic, geologic, and recreational resources. This road passes over rocks laid down a billion years ago. Pull off at Red Fleet State Park (named for the sailing "fleet" of red rock surrounding the water) to see a dinosaur trackway dating back 200 million years. As the road continues its rise, the surroundings turn green and sharp eyes will see fabulous birds, deer, elk and moose.

Thirty-five miles north of Vernal is the junction of US-191 and SR-44. From this point, you may turn northeast onto US-191 to access Flaming Gorge Dam and Visitor Center. Open year-round, the visitor center has a self-guided tour that takes you, via elevator, down into the heart of the million cubic yards of concrete that comprise the dam. As you continue to the Wyoming border, you have a great view of Flaming Gorge (named for its slash of red cliffs).

Large Photo: The deep teal color of Flaming Gorge Reservoir — Tom Till
Top Left Photo: The red cliffs of Flaming Gorge, Flaming Gorge NRA — Tom Till

If you choose to turn west onto SR-44 you will be heading toward the town of Manila. Four miles from the junction is the turnoff to Red Canyon Overlook and Visitor Center, which provides a stunning view of Red Canyon and the Green River that runs through it, spread out 1,500 feet below. Accessible about 18 miles from the junction is Sheep Creek Canyon Geologic Area and another great overview of Flaming Gorge. This area sustained some excruciating earth rotations two-and-a-half billion years ago, and the result is some fantastical formations. Manila is a six-mile drive from Sheep Creek Junction, completing the Byway.

What is the one-way, no-stops drive time?
If you travel the Byway directly from Vernal to Manila with no stops, allow one hour and 45 minutes to cover the 67 miles. Plan for extra time to accommodate photo stops and side trips.

For more information and a brochure:
Call Dinosaurland Travel Office at 435-789-6932, or the Vernal Ranger District office at 435-789-1181.

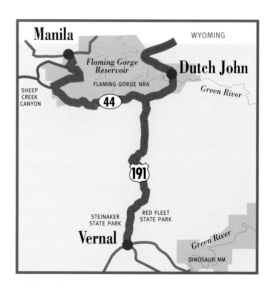

INDIAN CANYON
Scenic Byway

US-191 from its junction
with US-6 (just north of Helper)
to Duchesne

How do I get there? The Byway follows an old Native American trail used for travel between Price Valley and the Uinta Basin. It can be accessed from either end – traveling from the south, continue on US-191/6 north through the town of Helper, and veer east at the junction of US-6 and US-191, remaining on US-191; traveling from the north, exit US-6 at its junction with US-191. This is a sharp turn and not well marked from this direction. Slow down and look for the road as soon as you see the power plant.

What can I see and do? Once you get off the primary route of US-191/6, the Byway narrows and travels along Willow Creek. You will see wide-open vistas and pass through the beginnings of the Roan and Book Cliff formations. Peaking at 9100-foot Indian Pass, the Byway passes through the Ashley National Forest and a unique display of rock formations. The vegetation here includes pinyon, juniper, aspen and Douglas fir. Elk and deer sightings are common. The contrasts of autumn foliage are particularly beautiful. From the summit, the road follows Indian Canyon through desert terrain bordering Indian Creek. At the Byway's end lies the town of Duchesne, settled in 1904.

The towns that frame the Byway are both fun stops. Helper is named for the "helper" train cars attached to the heavily laden coal trains, before they make their arduous trip up Price Canyon. The town has a local history and mining museum, and in winter is famous for the "electric light parade," a two-night event when a couple of dozen floats, lit with thousands of tiny lights, make their way up Main Street. Duchesne has a visitor center in town, and its nearby reservoir, Starvation State Park, is popular with sailors and fishermen.

What is the one-way, no-stops drive time? The Byway has notably steep grades and is approximately 46 miles long. Driving time is about one hour.

For more information: Call Castle Country Tourism at 435-637-3009, or the Duchesne Ranger District office at 435-781-5200.

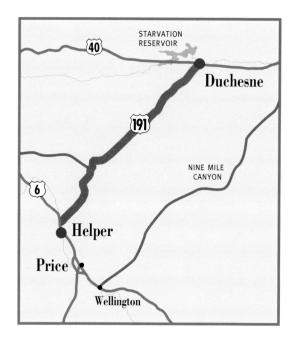

Inset Photo: The cliffs of Indian Canyon hide ancient rock art – Frank Jensen
Large Photo: Remnants of a not too distant Utah past – Frank Jensen

THE ENERGY LOOP:
HUNTINGTON & ECCLES CANYONS

National Scenic Byway
AMERICA'S
BYWAYS

SR-31 from Huntington
to Fairview;
SR-264 and SR-96 from
Fairview to Colton

How do I get there? The Energy Loop is a connection of two canyons – Huntington Canyon and Eccles Canyon, which together comprise the heart of Utah's energy production country. It can be accessed from either end – from the north at Colton off Highway 6, or from the south off SR-10 in Huntington.

What is there to see and do? These winding roadways begin in the east and western valleys below the Wasatch Plateau and reach elevations of over 10,000 feet, dissecting the pristine beauty of the Manti-La Sal National Forest. You will see and learn about prehistoric rock art, Native American history, early Spanish exploration routes, architecture of early settlers and the hardships of the first generation of the coal mining and railroad industries. The varieties of geologic strata provide a constantly changing landscape making the drive exhilarating any season of the year. This Byway is recognized by the Federal Highway Administration as a National Scenic Byway; one of America's premiere driving roads.

Large Photo: Babbling waters, Huntington Creek in Huntington Canyon – Jerry Sintz
Inset Photo: Scofield cemetery stands witness to early mining hardships – UTC
Far Right Photo: Scofield Reservoir is a year-round sportsman destination – Tom Till

The Byway starts in Huntington, home of scenic Huntington State Park, a landscaped park with picnic, camping and boating facilities. Departing from Huntington on SR-31, you will start the trip in arid Castle Valley, at the edge of the dramatic San Rafael Swell Desert. The route gradually winds through the Manti-La Sal National Forest to the town of Fairview. The views include jewel-like high elevation lakes, diverse vegetation, and vertical cliffs and escarpments. Recreation highlights are picnicking, camping, and fishing in lakes, reservoirs and streams. This is famed coal country, and you'll see several coal-fired energy generating projects.

Ten miles from Fairview is the turnoff to Eccles Canyon. This section of the Energy Loop Byway travels the Wasatch Plateau towards Clear Creek, and then on to Colton. Driving past working coalmine fields and the fishing haven of Electric Lake, the Byway eventually connects with Scofield Reservoir State Park. The reservoir is popular year-round; for boaters and fishermen in summer, and ice-fishers in winter. The park grooms miles of trails in winter for cross-country skiers and snowmobilers. Nearby is the historic mining town of Scofield. The Scofield Cemetery stands witness to the mining disasters which devastated the one-time boom town.

What is the one-way, no-stops drive time?

The total mileage for the two canyons is about 85 miles and requires at least four hours' drive time.

For more information:

Call Castle Country Tourism at 435-637-3009.

NEBO LOOP
National Scenic Byway

Uinta National Forest road 015 from Payson City to its junction with SR-132 (just east of Nephi); continuing on SR-132 to Nephi

How do I get there? You can access Nebo Loop from either its south or its north entrance. If you are traveling from the south, exit I-15 at Nephi exit 225. Follow SR-132 to the signed entrance to Nebo Loop. If you are traveling from the north, exit I-15 at Payson and follow the signs through town to the Peteetneet Academy and Nebo Loop.

What is there to see and do? This well-signed Byway is a winding drive between the cities of Payson

and Nephi. The road climbs to 9,000 feet and crosses the Uinta National Forest providing stunning views of Utah Valley, the surrounding Wasatch, and the dramatic wrap-around vistas of 11,877-foot Mt. Nebo, the highest peak in the rugged and beautiful Wasatch Range. Nebo Loop is designated a National Scenic Byway by the Federal Highway Administration, recognizing it as one of the premiere driving roads in America.

The Byway is a photographer's dream with many overlooks and wildlife viewing opportunities. The brilliant fall foliage of the Uinta National Forest is hard to match anywhere in the nation.

Along the way, there are numerous campgrounds, trail systems and popular horseback riding areas. Take time to pull off at the dozen interpretive sites – and learn about the unique history, geology and recreation in the area. Six stunning overlooks have viewing scopes. A unique scenic feature is the Devil's Kitchen Geologic Interest Site with picnic facilities, a paved trail and observation deck. The eroded sandstone

formation's startling red color adds contrast to the mountain greenery found through the rest of the Byway.

The Payson Lakes Recreation Area, 12 miles south of Payson, offers hiking on paved trails, improved picnic areas, camping and excellent fishing. The Byway also provides trail access into the Mount Nebo Wilderness Area.

What is the one-way, no-stops drive time?
The 32-mile Byway takes about one and one-half hours to complete. Heavy snow closes the road in winter.

Large Photo: Red maple reflections at Maple Lake — Mel Lewis
Inset Photo: Mt. Nebo, the highest peak in the Wasatch Range — Tom Till

For more information: Call Mountainland Travel Region at 801-229-3800, or the Uinta National Forest office at 801-342-5100. A brochure and map are available, as well as a 45-minute audio tape describing 24 markers and points of interest along the road. Scenic Nebo Loop has its own internet page. You may view it at www.mountainland.org/scenicbyways.

UPPER COLORADO RIVER
Scenic Byway

SR-128 from Moab
to its junction with I-70
(just west of Cisco)

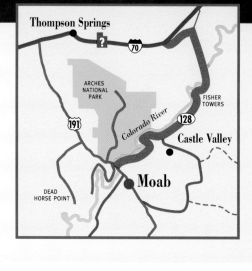

How do I get there? The Byway travels northeast from the town of Moab. It travels through a fabulous red rock canyon, carved out over a millennium by the Colorado River, which still travels its base. In addition to beautiful scenery, the Byway serves as a connecting route for motorists going to or from Moab and the nearby National Parks and BLM recreation sites.

What is there to see and do? The first major feature you'll see is about three miles from Moab, called Negro Bill Canyon. This canyon is named for William Granstaff, who ran cattle in the canyon during pioneer days. It's well worth your time to take a four-hour side trip and explore the canyon – a two-mile hiking trail leads to Morning Glory Natural Bridge.

Back on the main road, about four miles from Negro Bill Canyon, the Byway passes the BLM Big Bend Campground and picnic area with its white sand beach. The next section of the road closely parallels the Colorado River, where between May and October you'll see rafting parties floating through the rapids. A ranch, located to the left as the road curves, has been the scene of several western movies.

Shortly after the ranch, the Byway moves away from the river and crosses a wide natural rock amphitheater. Several miles past Castle Valley Junction, you will view famous Castle Rock, the finger-like spire to the southwest, which has been the setting for several films and commercials. Ahead are the crumbling mudstone ramparts of Fisher Towers. A side road leads to a campground and hiking trail at the base of the towers.

Eight miles east of Fisher Towers, the Byway crosses the mighty Colorado River near the historic Dewey Suspension Bridge built in 1916 and used until 1986. The bridge is on the National Register of Historic Places and you can get a great view from a roadside turnout. Beyond the bridge, the Byway briefly follows the Colorado River and then travels through open desert country to I-70 at the west Cisco interchange.

What is the one-way, no stops drive time?
The 44-mile long Byway can be traveled in a little over an hour.

For more information:
Call Canyonlands Travel Region at 435-259-1370.

*Large Photo: Last light on Fisher Towers and the peaks of the La Sal mountains
is reflected in the Colorado– Bill Crnkovich
Bottom Left Photo: Red rock walls and muddy water – Mel Lewis*

POTASH-LOWER COLORADO RIVER
Scenic Byway

SR-279 (junctions with US-191 three miles north of Moab) through Meander Canyon past Jug Handle Arch to the end of the pavement near the Potash Plant

How do I get there? Three miles north of Moab, US-191 junctions with SR-279. Turn south onto the Potash Road. The Byway follows the Colorado River through a meandering canyon for 17 miles to Jug Handle Arch.

What can I see and do? The Moab area is well known for its abundance of Native American rock art. Two "Indian Writings" signs along this Scenic Byway identify the locations of several petroglyph panels (figures carved on cliff faces) with individual carvings depicting symbolic animals and human-like figures.

Farther along the road, another sign points out the location of a large rock above the highway where you will see a set of dinosaur tracks. The BLM has made these historic sites easy for you to see and enjoy, but please don't touch – even the slightest oil residue will stain the rocks. These sites are extremely vulnerable and fragile, and left alone they will continue to educate future generations.

After the dinosaur tracks, the Byway passes Corona Arch trailhead. If you have an extra two hours, this is a wonderful side trip. A 1.5-mile hiking trail leads to Corona, which has a 140-foot by 105-foot opening, as well as nearby Bow Tie Arch.

Near the end of the road another sign points out the descriptively named Jug Handle Arch. This arch, which is just above the highway, is 46 feet high and just three feet wide.

Shortly beyond Jug Handle Arch, the canyon widens, and you may well gasp with delight at the sight of the sheer cliffs below Dead Horse Point State Park, visible in the distance. The paved highway ends at the Moab Salt Plant where potash, a mineral used as a fertilizer, is extracted by flushing large volumes of

water through an extensive system of tunnels and then evaporating the water in ponds. From the end of the Byway, drivers with high clearance vehicles can continue on a dirt road to Canyonlands National Park.

What is the one-way, no stops drive time? The Byway is 17 miles in, and 17 miles out. For most motorists this is a one-way, in-and-out drive – continuing on the road will most likely require a four-wheel drive vehicle. Allow two hours for the 34-mile round-trip drive to Jug Handle Arch.

For more information:
Call Canyonlands Travel Region at 435-259-1370.

Large Photo: A lazy summer morning dawns on the Colorado – Tom Till

Inset Photo: Jug Handle Arch along Potash Road – Jerry Sintz

INDIAN CREEK CORRIDOR
Scenic Byway

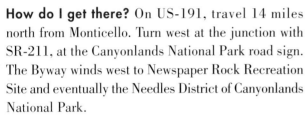

SR-211 (junctions with US-191 fourteen miles north of Monticello) to its terminus in the Needles section of Canyonlands National Park

How do I get there? On US-191, travel 14 miles north from Monticello. Turn west at the junction with SR-211, at the Canyonlands National Park road sign. The Byway winds west to Newspaper Rock Recreation Site and eventually the Needles District of Canyonlands National Park.

What can I see and do? The route traverses high sage plains before plunging down through a series of tight turns to Indian Creek and the pull-off to Newspaper Rock Recreation Site. Managed by the Monticello Field Office of the BLM, Newspaper Rock is a 50-foot high rock face covered with petroglyphs from several distinct cultures. From prehistory through frontier days, people felt the need to make their mark at this timeworn junction, and the result is a fascinating and crowded mix of messages that cover the huge rock slab. Interpretive signage describes the various ages of different figures.

From Newspaper Rock the Byway passes through beautiful Indian Creek Canyon, where you might spot rock climbers hanging tightly to the towering red walls. The road skirts Dugout Ranch, one of the earliest and largest private cattle ranches in the area and now owned and operated by The Nature Conservancy. The Byway continues another dozen-or-so miles to the Needles District of Canyonlands National Park.

The Byway officially ends here, continuing into the National Park you are entering a fee area. In the Park a visitor center, campground, and six-mile scenic drive are accessible via a paved road. Look for the distinctive wooden shoe formation. There are two short, easy hikes in the area. Roadside Ruin takes you to an ancient Native American storehouse. Cave Spring Trail takes you to an old cowboy camp. Numerous foot trails and

four-wheel drive routes lead into the backcountry, among them the challenging Elephant Hill route.

What is the one-way, no-stops drive time? The Byway is 18 miles in and 18 miles out. This is a one-way, in-and-out road, and the 35 mile roundtrip takes about two hours. You can easily spend a half-day or more exploring the area.

For more information: Call San Juan County Tourism Visitor Services at 435-587-3235 or 800-574-4386.

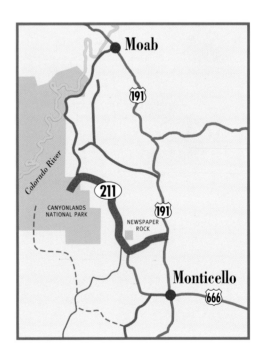

Large Photo: Ancient Newspaper Rock art – Jim Maire
Small Photo: South Six Shooter Peak – Tom Till

BICENTENNIAL - TRAIL OF THE ANCIENTS
Scenic Byway

SR-95 from Hanksville to Blanding; includes the side trip on SR-275 to Natural Bridges Nat'l Monument; south on US-191 from Blanding to Bluff; and east on SR-163 and SR-262 to the Colorado border.

How do I get there? The Byway can be accessed from either end: from Hanksville at the junction of SR 24 and SR-95; or from the Colorado border at SR-262 just east of Aneth.

What can I see and do? The landscape on the Byway is diverse. You will criss-cross the major attractions in southeastern Utah, from the "moonscape" landforms near Hanksville, to the sparkling blue waters of Lake Powell; from massive natural bridges to red rock monoliths; from dinosaurs and prehistoric humans to pioneers… and on to the Colorado border.

Begin your trip in the pioneer town of Hanksville. Just south, the Byway skirts reminders of the Gold Rush and pioneer eras. As it enters Glen Canyon National Recreation Area it winds through magnificent red gorges on its approach to the distant blue of

Lake Powell. A pull-off overlook offers an expansive view of the northern end of the lake. At the Dirty Devil River the road spans a deep rock gorge and at Hite another bridge crosses the Narrow Canyon of the Colorado River.

About 45 miles southeast of Hite Marina, the off-shoot road of SR-275 enjoins the Byway and winds through pinion and juniper forest to Natural Bridges National Monument. The monument contains the world's largest display of natural bridges. A nine-mile loop accesses viewpoints for each of the three bridges, which nature has carved from 225-million year-old Cedar Mesa sandstone.

Back on the main road, SR-95 travels east past BLM's Mule Canyon Indian Ruin, which offers easy access to a partially restored prehistoric ruin. Mule Canyon is accessible for the physically challenged and offers interpretive signing. Continuing east, the road climbs up and through Comb Ridge, once a formidable rock barrier to east/west travel. From Comb Ridge you can side trip on trails leading to biking, four-wheeling, or hiking opportunities. East of Comb Ridge an "Indian Ruin" sign marks the trail to the Butler Wash Cliff Dwelling overlook. A one-mile hike here crosses sandstone and winds through juniper and cactus to an overlook of the ruin, with helpful interpretive signage. At the junction of SR-95 and US-191, the Byway heads north to the town of Blanding. There are several worth-

while stops here, including the Blanding Dinosaur Museum and Edge of the Cedars State Park – both interpret ancient life in the area.

From Blanding, head south on US-191 to Bluff, a charming pioneer-era town on the San Juan River. From Bluff, head southeast on SR-163 and SR-262. At the town of Aneth you will see signs for Hovenweep National Monument. This is a wonderful side trip where you can walk among ancient towers from a long-ago culture. Be sure and check locally for road conditions, however, and make sure you pack plenty of water. There are no visitor services available at Hovenweep. Back on the Byway, continue southeast to the Colorado border and on to Mesa Verde National Park.

What is the one-way, no-stops drive ?
This Byway is 164 miles long. Travel time is about four hours.

For more information and a brochure on "Trail of the Ancients": Call San Juan County Tourism Visitor Services at 435-587-3235 or 800-574-4386.

Note: The "Trail of the Ancients" interprets the major transportation pathway of ancient people, and continues a four-state loop through Colorado, New Mexico and Arizona.

Large Photo: Hidden ancient cliff dwelling, near the Colorado River – Tom Till

Inset Photo: On the Trail of the Ancients, Hwy 95 near Hite – Mel Lewis

MONUMENT VALLEY TO BLUFF
Scenic Byway

US-163 from the
Utah/Arizona border
to Bluff

How do I get there? From the Arizona border, Scenic Byway 163 travels northeast through Monument Valley and on to the historic community of Bluff.

What is there to see and do? Monument Valley has possibly the most photographed set of rocks in the world. As you approach the Valley, from miles away, you will see the beautiful monolithic formations that have been the setting for countless western movies and advertisements. People from all over the world feel at home here because the surroundings are so familiar.

All the land you see around you is Navajo Tribal

Land. If you exit the Byway and take the short side trip to the Monument Valley Visitor Center, you will pass the storefronts of dozens of Native Americans selling jewelry, souvenirs and food.

A fee is charged to enter the Monument's Visitor Center area, where you will find a restaurant, gift shop and great views. Look for formations named mittens, elephant, camel, three sisters, eagle, and many more. If you wish to get into the Valley and up close to the rock monuments, you will need to hire a guide. Guide services are available at the visitor center.

Back on the main road and across the highway is Goulding's Trading Post, which has a large motel, restaurant, and a gift shop.

Large Photo: View from Mitchell Mesa, Monument Valley Tribal Park, AZ– Tom Till
Inset Photo: Many of the Bluff pioneer houses have been restored – Frank Jensen
Top Right Photo: Butler Wash petroglyphs along the San Juan River – Tom Till

Continuing north on US-163, you will climb to 5,209-foot Monument Pass. As the Byway leaves the northern end of Monument Valley you will pass Alhambra, a volcanic core that stands prominently next to the road.

The next settlement on the Byway is Mexican Hat, named for the sombrero-shaped rock formation visible from the road. In the middle of town the road crosses the San Juan River on an historic suspension bridge. Past Mexican Hat, a worthwhile side trip is SR-316 that leads to the Great Goosenecks of the San Juan River, a small park with a huge overlook into the gorge where the river has carved twists and turns into the landscape.

Another popular side trip is a 17-mile loop drive on native surface road through BLM's Valley of the Gods. The road is well-marked from the Byway. This trip is perfect for mountain biking or high clearance vehicles. Home to sandstone monoliths that rise from the valley floor, this rugged and remote landscape rivals nearby Monument Valley.

Near the Byway's end, the road crosses Comb Ridge. Look for the sign to BLM's recreation site and campground Sand Island (not a real island, but a lot of sand) to see an impressive petroglyph panel on the cliff along the San Juan River. Five images of Kokopelli, the humpbacked flute player of ancient mythology, are found among many other figures on the panel.

Three miles up the road this Byway ends in the town of Bluff, the oldest pioneer settlement in southeast Utah. The Victorian-era homes here were some of the state's grandest at the close of the 19th century. US-163 continues on to the Colorado border.

What is the one-way, no-stops drive time?

Allow two hours for this 45-mile Scenic Byway. Plan extra time to enjoy side trips and photo stops.

For more information:

Call San Juan County Tourism Visitor Services at 435-587-3235 or 800-574-4386.

FISHLAKE
Scenic Byway

SR-25 from SR-24
to Gooseberry/Fremont Road

How do I get there? The Byway is reached by traveling northwest on SR-24 in Loa to the junction with SR-25.

What is there to see and do? This is a trek through mountains and meadows of the Fishlake National Forest to two of the most scenic and popular fishing spots in the state. Early on, you will experience a change in terrain from sagebrush and occasional trees

to high mountain aspen, shimmering in their summer greenery or blazing fall foliage. Wildlife is abundant along the way. Deer and elk are a common sight among the trees, and moose were recently reintroduced to the area. Mountain lions make their homes in the surrounding mountains, but are rarely seen. At Fish Lake a variety of waterfowl and birds are established including golden and bald eagles. The fishing is excellent at both Fish Lake and Johnson Reservoir.

Fish Lake, occupying a basin ringed by steep-sided mountains, owes its existence to the combined geological forces of millions of years. Resorts, day-use areas, and campgrounds are located all along this route.

Look for the unusual rock monuments, found along the west end of SR-25, which were built over a period of 40 years by a local sheepherder.

What is the one-way, no-stops drive time?
This Byway is 13 miles long and requires approximately 45 minutes.

For more information:
Call Wayne County Tourism at 435-425-3939, or Fishlake National Forest at 435-896-9233.

Large Photo: Utah quakies frame Fish Lake reflections – Frank Jensen

Inset Photo: Mt Terrill, Fishlake NF – John P. George

CAPITOL REEF COUNTRY
Scenic Byway

SR-24 from Loa
to Hanksville

How do I get there? The road meanders southeast from the I-70/US-89 junction south of Salina to Hanksville and then north to I-70 west of Green River. The portion between the towns of Loa and Hanksville is designated as a Scenic Byway.

What is there to see and do? The Byway-designated portion of this route runs through the heart of Capitol Reef National Park. The road also accesses Fishlake National Forest, Goblin Valley State Park, the San Rafael Swell and the most remote areas of Canyonlands National Park.

Descending from rolling sagebrush desert and 8,000-foot elevations near Fish Lake, the Byway plunges through high valley farmlands into Capitol Reef National Park. With easy access to the park visitor center and campground, the Byway hugs the banks of the Fremont River as it flows past pioneer orchards and the gorges and red rock formations of Capitol Reef, named for the white rock dome resembling the nation's capitol building.

After exiting the park, the route moves east through the stark beauty of Mancos shale hills and past abandoned settlements of hardy Mormon pioneers. Thirty-seven miles east of Capitol Reef, at Hanksville, SR-24 shoots north for another 22 miles to junctions leading to Goblin Valley State Park and Canyonlands National Park. At the west junction, seven miles of paved road and four miles of oiled road lead to the "goblins"; a forest of eroded sandstone shapes. To the east, about 60 miles of graded dirt road lead into the colorful Maze District of Canyonlands National Park. Hiking boots and a four-wheel drive vehicle are strongly recommended for this road section.

As SR-24 continues on to I-70, the enormous, multi-hued San Rafael Reef is prominent to the west.

What is the one-way, no-stops drive time?
This 162-mile journey takes about four hours.

For more information:
Call Wayne County Tourism at 435-425-3939.

Large Photo: Ghosts of Caineville – Tom Till

Inset: Painted Desert, Capitol Reef NP – Frank Jensen

41

HWY 12 - A JOURNEY THROUGH TIME
Scenic Byway

SR-12 from its junction
with US-89 (near Panguitch)
to the town of Torrey

How do I get there? The Byway may be accessed
from either end. Traveling from the south, exit US-89
at SR-12. This exit is a few miles north of the town of
Hatch. Traveling from the north, exit SR-24 at the
town of Torrey, and head south on SR-12.

What is there to see and do? This is one of the most
spectacular drives in the West, passing through Bryce
Canyon National Park, Grand Staircase-Escalante
National Monument, over Boulder Mountain in the Dixie
National Forest to its conclusion near the entrance of
Capitol Reef National Park.

Beginning off US-89 south of Panguitch, the
Byway heads east through Red Canyon in the Dixie

National Forest and rises
in elevation toward Bryce
Canyon National Park. At
Bryce, a side trip on the
18 mile-long park road
(SR-63) begins 15 miles
east of the SR-12 and
US-89 junction and leads
south through the park to views of hoodoo-filled
amphitheaters and cool meadows and forests. A fee is
required in the National Park.

Back on the main route, the Byway passes through
the northern portions of Bryce Canyon on the way to
the town of Tropic. A small community rich in pioneer
heritage, Tropic is typical of the other small towns on
SR-12 east of Bryce Canyon. Near the town of
Cannonville is the northern boundary of the Grand
Staircase-Escalante National Monument. A Visitor
Center in Cannonville will help you experience the
National Monument as well as local culture past and
present. A seven-mile paved road leads south from
Cannonville to colorful Kodachrome Basin State Park
(fee required) for a delightful side trip.

One mile west of the town of Escalante is Escalante State Park – a petrified forest featuring colorful deposits of mineralized wood and dinosaur bones. At the park boundary is Wide Hollow Reservoir, offering boating and fishing. This town also borders the Grand Staircase-Escalante National Monu-

ment, and has the Escalante Interagency Visitor Center, which will help you plan your time in this incredible area.

The road continues through the Escalante canyons with panoramic views over miles of colorful slick rock. After crossing the Escalante River, you can picnic at BLM's Calf Creek Campground, and take a wonderful, moderately strenuous, six-mile round-trip trail to Lower Calf Creek Falls, which cascades 126 feet over Navajo sandstone.

Nearing the town of Boulder, SR-12 twists and turns through the Hogsback, a section where cliffs drop steeply into narrow canyons on both sides of the highway. In Boulder a museum and remnants of a prehistoric Native American village at Anasazi State Park take visitors back in time thousands of years.

Following the summit of Boulder Mountain, the Byway travels a spectacular forested course where views of colorful Capitol Reef National Park, the Circle Cliffs and the Henry Mountains are framed by the trees of the Dixie National Forest. Autumn on Boulder Mountain means golden aspen groves punctuated by pines. From Boulder Mountain, the road drops to the Byway's end in the farming town of Torrey near the entrance to Capitol Reef National Park.

What is the one-way, no-stops drive time?
Highway 12, known for some of the state's most varied scenery, is 122 miles long and takes at least four hours' travel time.

For more information:
Call Garfield County at 435-676-8826.

Large Photo: Oasis in the desert, Calf Creek Falls – Frank Jensen
Left Text Inset Photo: An autumn drive over Boulder Mountain – J. Spence Kinard
Right Text Photo: Sinking Ship, Bryce NP – Tom Till

MARKAGUANT HIGH PLATEAU
Scenic Byway

SR-14 from Cedar City
to its junction with US-89
(at Long Valley Junction)

How do I get there? Access the Byway at either end–from Cedar City and I-15 on the west; or Long Valley Junction and US-89 on the east.

What is there to see and do? SR-14 is one of southern Utah's most traveled highways, climbing through Cedar Canyon and into the Dixie National Forest. Once you leave I-15, the Byway climbs steeply

through a narrow canyon looking into Ashdown Gorge, where sheer cliffs tower on both sides of the canyon. In the fall this area is brilliant with red maples and golden oaks. As you enter the Dixie National Forest, the view looks into a sand-cut amphitheater of bright red limestone in contrast with green trees linking the edges and the skyline. Brian Head Resort, a year round alpine recreation area, can be accessed from this Byway on SR- 148/143.

At the canyon summit, a parking area beside the road at Zion Overlook provides a panoramic view of Kolob Terrace and the distant towers and buttes of Zion National Park.

SR-14 tops out at 9,900 feet, then continues across Cedar Mountain to several points of interest including Navajo Lake, a favorite for fishing, camping and photography. The three-and-a-half mile-long lake is drained by sinkholes where water from inlets dramatically disappears into the ground.

Several miles east of Navajo Lake is a popular summer home area and the fishing waters of Duck Creek. A short side trip to Strawberry Point provides a beautiful view of the red rock cliffs of Zion National Park.

Throughout the landscape along the Byway you'll see huge lava beds and layers of volcanic rock that attest to the region's igneous past. Adventurers may want to travel the gravel road side trip to Mammoth Cave. The "cave" is actually a lava tube – an air space in the lava that is big enough to walk around in. Watch for signs to the Cave – it is not easy to find.

What is the one-way, no-stops driving time?
The Byway is 40 miles long and takes one hour to travel.

For more information:
Call the Iron County Tourism office at 435-586-5124.

Large Photo: The jeweled waters of Navajo Lake – Frank Jensen
Inset Photo: Gnarled juniper on the Markaguant Plateau – Tom Till

CEDAR BREAKS
Scenic Byway

SR-148 between SR-14 and SR-143 (near Cedar City)

How do I get there? Traveling on SR-14, head east of Cedar City for about 15 miles, and turn north at the junction of SR-148. The Byway covers the entirety of SR-148, passing through flower-filled meadows to Cedar Breaks National Monument.

What is there to see and do? You will drive along through lovely, open meadows of the Dixie National Forest – suddenly Cedar Breaks National Monument opens it massive earthen jaws and takes your breath away. This is a huge natural amphitheater, more than 2,000 feet deep and three miles from rim to rim. Millions of years of wind, rain and snow have eroded the walls into carved spirals with dazzling multi-colored ridges and rock formations. Especially in morning and evening they glow with hues of orange, coral, rose and white.

Surrounding the bowl, and adding a wonderful contrast, are small stands of bristlecone pine and juniper. A five-mile scenic drive around the perimeter has four pull-off lookout points. A lovely, moderate hike is the two-mile Alpine Pond Trail. There is a visitor center and campground. A fee is required at the national monument.

From Cedar Breaks, SR-148 continues north for four miles to its junction with SR-143.

What is the one-way, no-stops drive time? This drive covers six miles and travel time is about 30 minutes. The Monument's visitor center is open from Memorial Day to Columbus Day. The Byway remains open until heavy snow forces its closure – usually around mid-November.

For more information: Call Cedar Breaks National Monument at 435-586-9451.

Large Photo: Point Supreme at sunset, Cedar Breaks NM – Tom Till
Inset Photo: Iced engelman spruce on the rim – Tom Till

BRIAN HEAD-PANGUITCH LAKE
Scenic Byway

SR-143 from Parowan
to Panguitch

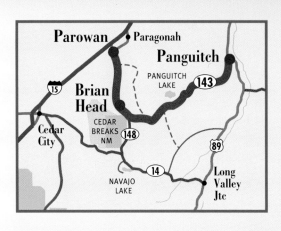

How do I get there? From Parowan and I-15, SR-143 moves southeast past Brian Head Resort, skirts Cedar Breaks National Monument, and passes through alpine stretches of the Dixie National Forest on its way to Panguitch.

What is there to see and do? The Byway climbs past the colorful Vermillion Cliffs, through Parowan Canyon, rises to forested heights of 10,000 feet, then drops down to Panguitch. The colored aspens and maples in mid-September make this a perfect autumn drive.

Brian Head Resort near 11,305-foot Brian Head Peak is located twelve miles southeast of Parowan. The town of Brian Head, (elevation 9,800 feet), is Utah's highest incorporated city. This is a year-round resort with a variety of lodging and dining facilities, shops, and recreational activities including skiing, snowboarding and snow tubing in the winter and hiking and mountain biking in the summer. Cedar Breaks National Monument on U-148 (see page 46 for Cedar Breaks Scenic Byway) is located three miles south of Brian Head.

About 20 miles east of Cedar Breaks, along SR-143, is Panguitch Lake, a popular summer and winter fishing spot and recreational area. The forests of the vast Markaguant Plateau surrounding Panguitch Lake are brilliant with autumn colors including yellow, orange and red aspen leaves that have drawn photographers from all over the country. Seventeen miles northeast of the lake is the town of Panguitch, noted for its distinctive late-1800s red brick houses. There was once a brick kiln in town, and every man that worked there received enough bricks to build a house.

What is the one-way, no-stops drive time? The Byway is 55 miles long. Because of some steep grades, allow one and one-half hours travel time. The road is open year-round, snow tires or chains are recommended during the winter months. The road is not plowed at night.

For more information: Call Iron County Tourism at 435-586-5124, or Garfield County at 435-676-8826.

Large Photo: Rock formations in Parowan Canyon — Frank Jensen
Bottom Left Photo: View west toward the Great Basin from Brian Head Peak — Tom Till

BEAVER CANYON
Scenic Byway

SR-153 from Beaver
to Elk Meadows Resort

How do I get there? From the town of Beaver, accessed directly off I-15, the Byway ascends east to the Tushar Mountain Range in Fishlake National Forest. The road terminates at Elk Meadows Ski and Summer Resort. Beaver Canyon is a one-way, in-and-out Byway.

What is there to see and do? Beaver Canyon is a hidden jewel, still mostly undiscovered by recreationists. It has excellent camping, hiking, mountain biking and hunting. Fishing is plentiful in mountain lakes and streams. In autumn the Canyon is resplendent with colorful aspens and maples. Winter activities include snowmobiling and cross-country skiing.

Elk Meadows Ski and Summer Resort, 17 miles east

of the town of Beaver, is nestled beneath 12,000-foot Mt. Holly and Delano Peak. The year-round resort has shops, restaurants, log cabins and condominiums. In winter the slopes are covered with Utah's signature "Greatest Snow on Earth," and are usually not crowded.

Not on the Byway, but nearby and worth mentioning, is Minersville State Park, 12 miles west of Beaver on SR-21. This reservoir has camping, great fishing, and sparkler stars at night.

What is the one-way, no-stops drive time?
The Beaver Canyon Scenic Byway is 17 miles long and takes 45 minutes to drive.

For more information: Call the Fishlake National Forest office in Richfield at 435-896-9233.

Large Photo: Bear Creek, Tushar Mountains, Fishlake NF – Frank Jensen
Text Inset Photo: Engelman spruce and golden rock in the Tushers – Jerry Sintz
Text Inset Photo: Mountain goats with Mt Belnap in the distance – Jerry Sintz

MT. CARMEL
Scenic Byway

US-89 from Kanab to
its junction with SR-12

How do I get there? One of Utah's most popular drives, the Byway travels from Kanab on the south to Red Canyon in the north and ascends southern Utah's Grand Staircase of vermillion, white and pink cliffs.

What is there to see and do? Kanab is nicknamed Utah's "Little Hollywood," because of the 70-plus movies that have been filmed here, from John Wayne westerns to *Planet of the Apes*.

From Kanab the Byway follows US-89 through Three Lakes Canyon and the Vermillion Cliffs, past several western movie locations, including Old Paria, built in 1963 for the movie *Sergeants Three*, and Johnson Canyon, where all of the outdoor scenes from the TV series *Gunsmoke* were filmed.

The road soon passes the turn off to Coral Pink Sand

Dunes State Park. This is a wild, other worldly place, and well worth a side trip. The sand is truly pink – the color of the inside of an exotic seashell. And there are truly dunes – tall hills of sand stretching as far as the eye can see. For several thousand years the surrounding colorful rock has been evolving into these dunes, and the result is extremely photogenic. There is a nature trail and a boardwalk that takes you out into the dunes. A fee is required at state parks.

Back on the Byway, a panoramic view unfolds of the White Cliffs and the majestic towers of Zion National Park. Next, you will descend to the east fork of the Virgin River at Mt. Carmel Junction. The road then winds through the green fields and orchards of Long

Valley and the towns of Mt. Carmel, Orderville and Glendale. A backdrop of yellow, red and white-banded cliffs are continually in view. North of Glendale, the highway leaves the canyon landscape and enters a forested mountain valley. The Pink Cliffs and formations reminiscent of Bryce Canyon appear at either side of the road. At Long Valley Junction, the Byway descends the wide mountain valley of the Sevier River through

Hatch to Red Canyon Junction and the beginning of SR-12. Trout-laden streams enter the valley from the west. Late afternoon views of the pink cliffs highlighted along the length of the valley are stunning.

What is the one-way, no-stops drive time?

This Byway is 60 miles long and requires one and one-half hours to complete.

For more information:

Call Kane County Visitor Information at 435-644-5033.

Large Photo: White cliffs of the Grand Staircase — Frank Jensen
Inset Photo: Four-wheeling at Coral Pink Sand Dunes State Park — Frank Jensen

ZION PARK
Scenic Byway

SR-9 from I-15 to
Mt. Carmel Junction

How do I get there? The Byway begins about nine miles north of St. George, exiting from I-15 at the signs indicating Hurricane city and Zion National Park.

What is there to see and do? The Byway passes first through the town of Hurricane, supposedly named after a whirlwind, that snapped the top off a settler's buggy and caused him to exclaim "Well, that was a hurricane!" Nearby is Quail Creek Reservoir State Park which is popular year-round for fishing and water recreation.

After passing through Hurricane, the road veers at LaVerkin and climbs to the crest of the Hurricane cliffs to offer a sweeping view of the Pine Valley Mountains. The Byway then winds through the valley of the Virgin River at the foot of Hurricane Mesa, Smithsonian Butte and the Eagle Crags.

You'll pass through the pioneer towns of Virgin and Rockville. If you like  ghost towns consider a side trip to Grafton. Cross the river at Rockville and head three and a half miles west where you will see the turn-off signs. Grafton is a well-preserved ghost town, and its cemetery just north of town is an interesting historical record.

Continuing on you will reach Springdale, the full-service town that caters to visitors at Zion National Park. There are many motels, restaurants and great shops here. The local giant screen theater shows films that interpret the West, and in summer the outdoor Tanner Amphitheater has nightly multimedia shows that showcase nature's wonders.

At Springdale's border is the main attraction of the Byway: Zion National Park. The Byway runs right through the heart of Zion, taking you past world famous formations and monoliths. A fee is charged in national parks. A must-see, six-mile side trip is Zion Canyon, which is considered "the true Zion experience." In this section of the Park you'll see towering sandstone cliffs comprising the Court of the Patriarchs, the Great White Throne and Angel's Landing. Each season this magnificent canyon takes on a new look with the reds, oranges and golds of autumn, an occasional dusting of snow in the winter and a miraculous variety of greens in summer.

From November to March visitors may drive their own vehicles into Zion Canyon. From April to October access into the Canyon is by a free shuttle bus. Park officials encourage you to park your car in Springdale, catch the town shuttle to the park, exit and walk across the bridge to the visitor center, and then re-board to enter the Canyon. The trip takes about 90 minutes round trip from the visitor center through Zion Canyon.

Back on the main road, you will see the Great Arch of Zion and pass through a long tunnel carved in the massive canyon walls. Completed in 1930 and an engineering marvel in its time, the tunnel does not easily accommodate large, modern vehicles. However, special regulations provide for safe passage, and large vehicles and motor homes are required to pay an escort fee to travel through the tunnel. Past the tunnel, the Byway traverses a unique landscape of petrified sand dunes to reach the park's east entrance. Be sure to notice Checkerboard Mesa, which is criss-crossed with cracks into a surprisingly geometric pattern.

The Byway continues to its terminus at Mt. Carmel Junction. From here you can head south to Kanab or north to Long Valley Junction.

What is the one-way, no-stops drive time?
The Byway is 54 miles long and travel time is about one and one-half hours.

For more information: Call St. George Area Visitor Information at 435-634-5747 or 800-869-6635.

Large Photo: The winding road from Springdale to Mt. Carmel — Frank Jensen
Inset Photo: Towers of the Virgin, at the entrance to Zion NP — Tom Till

ZION
NATIONAL
PARK

🛡15 LaVerkin

9

Hurricane

Springdale

Mt. Carmel

🛡89

89

Harrisburg
Jtc

59

Hildale

Kanab

ARIZONA

KOLOB FINGERS ROAD
Scenic Byway

Kolob Fingers Road -
Junctions with I-15
18 miles south of Cedar City

How do I get there? Travel I-15 about 18 miles south of Cedar City; at Exit 40 turn east to enter the colorful Kolob Canyons section of Zion National Park.

What is there to see and do? A year-round visitor center is located at the canyon road entrance – stop by for a self-guided brochure that describes park features. A fee is required in National Parks.

An ancient stream carved these spectacular canyons from the stone of the Kolob Terrace. The road climbs through several switchbacks on its ascent to the top. The spectacular "finger canyons" are rugged, narrow, and colored in vibrant shades of red.

Several hiking trails, with different levels of difficulty,

begin at the main road. The trail to Kolob Arch, probably the largest freestanding arch in the world, starts at Lee's Pass on the Kolob Fingers Road. This 14 mile round-trip hike is strenuous and takes about eight hours. It is not recommended for the summer months.

The Byway features pull outs with splendid overlooks and signs with geologic information. Don't miss the viewpoint at the terminus of Kolob Terrace Road, which overlooks the cliffs of North Creek.

What is the one-way, no-stops drive time? From the visitor center at the base of the Byway to the summit is approximately five miles and requires 30 minutes.

For more information:
Call Zion National Park information at 435-772-3256.

Large Photo: Blue sky and Kolob Arch, Kolob Canyons, Zion NP– Frank Jensen
Inset Photo: Red rock, purple shadows and green juniper – Frank Jensen

DEAD HORSE POINT MESA
Scenic Byway

SR-313,
nine miles north of Moab
off US-191

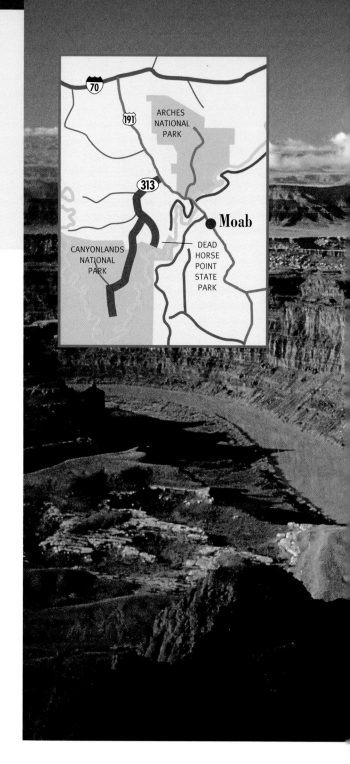

How do I get there? To travel the road, head north from Moab on US-191. After about nine miles look for the "Dead Horse Point State Park" sign and turn left.

What is there to see and do? The view from Dead Horse Point is one of the most photographed scenic vistas in the world – the panorama of the Colorado River Canyon. Grandview looks down on the Needles and Maze sections of Canyonlands National Park, as well as the Green and Colorado river canyons.

At the start of the spectacular Scenic Byway, you will pass through 14 miles of BLM's incredible red rock canyon country. Pull-offs along the way interpret the geology, archeology and scenery seen from the highway. Look for Seven Mile Canyon, the massive Monitor and Merrimac buttes, views of the San Rafael Reef and the Henry Mountains. The Gemini Bridges Trail is popular with four-wheelers and leads to two natural bridges.

After 14 miles you will come to a fork in the road. The road is well-signed. Turn left for the short drive to Dead Horse Point State Park. From the parking lot a short walk takes you to the overlook. Hands down, this is one of the premier views in the world. You'll see (way down!) the landscapes and colors created by the Colorado River over several millennia, with valleys and mountain ranges in the further distance. The name "Dead Horse" comes from the natural "corral" formed by the narrow-necked plateau which houses the state park. The legend goes that a hundred years ago, cowboys left horses here to pasture, didn't leave enough water, and forgot about them until it was too late.

Back on the main road, the Island in the Sky Road goes for another 16 miles until it reaches Grandview Point. Again, a short walk from the parking lot takes you to an overlook and a spectacular view of red rock so beautiful it has been given protection as a national park. On a clear day (cloudy weather will limit your view) you will see hundreds of miles of nature, unencumbered by human intrusions. You can leave the overlook for a short walk over red rock, which offers different vantage points.

For most drivers, this road, from its separate viewpoints, is a one-way, in-and-out drive. There is access to Island in the Sky section of Canyonlands National Park from Grandview Point.

What is the one-way, no-stops drive time? From the visitor information kiosk at the base of the Byway to the summit is approximately five miles and requires 30 minutes.

For more information: Call Moab Area Travel Council at 435-259-1370 or 800-635-6622.

Large Photo: Breath-taking! The view from Dead Horse Point State Park — Frank Jensen
Inset Photo: Claret cup cactus blossom — Frank Jensen

LEGACY PARKWAY

North Salt Lake to Farmington

The 14-mile Legacy Parkway is a unique concept juxtaposing humans and their automobiles with wildlife and their wetlands. In the fall of 2004, the four-lane road will connect major metropolitan areas in northern Utah, passing through the coastal ecosystem created by the Great Salt Lake. The drive offers extraordinary views of Antelope Island, the Great Salt Lake and the Wasatch Mountains.

A trail system for walkers, joggers, roller-bladers and cyclists runs parallel to the Parkway, separated from the road by fence, berms and foliage.

Directly west of the road is the 2,098-acre Legacy Nature Preserve, home to many species of shorebirds and other wildlife and a vital stopover for millions of migrating birds.

Heaven's Palette, a Great Salt Lake Sunset – Steve Greenwood

HERITAGE HIGHWAY 89

SR-89 from Kanab to Fairview

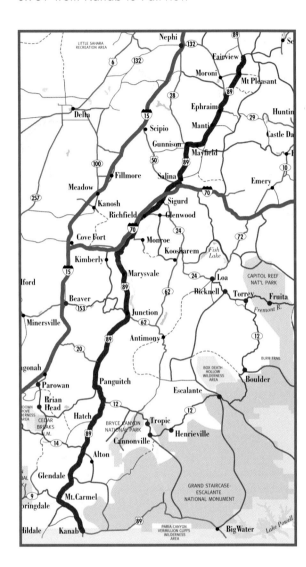

The artisans and business owners along this route are dedicated to offering tourists an authentic Western experience. They have identified five separate Heritage Areas, each with distinct geographic, cultural and historic characteristics. In addition to learning about local lore, visitors can see heritage sites and events, buy and eat heritage products and food.

For more information and a map call 435-462-2456 or visit http://heritageproducts.utah.org.

UTAH NATIONAL PARKS HWY

US-89/SR-40

(See Special Highways, Official Utah State Map)

If you love redrock and spectacular panoramas, this is the trip for you. This route zigzags across the vast landscapes of southern Utah, delivering you to all five of Utah's national parks, and several of our national monuments and forests. The exact route can be traced on the Utah State Highway Map.

Utah National Parks Highway connects:

Zion National Park

Cedar Breaks National Monument

Red Canyon

Bryce Canyon National Park

Grand Staircase-Escalante National Monument

Dixie National Forest

Capitol Reef National Park

Glen Canyon National Recreation Area (Lake Powell)

Natural Bridges National Monument

Canyonlands National Park

Arches National Park

Along the Scenic Drive, Capitol Reef National Park – Frank Jensen

DINOSAUR DIAMOND PREHISTORIC HIGHWAY

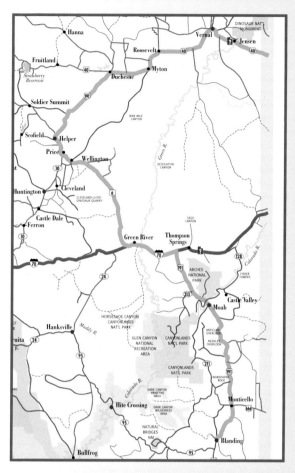

Starting from Utah's Blanding, north through Moab, Price and Vernal, then a return trip south through Colorado's Dinosaur, Rangely and Fruita – this road links important dinosaur related sites.

This 512-mile route creates a "diamond" pattern on the map, traveling back roads through Utah and Colorado. This was once the world's "Jurassic Park," a breathtaking world of dinosaurs that roamed the region for million of years and then disappeared. Today dinosaur enthusiasts come from all over the world to look in awe. Travelers will find museums, active dig sites and rock art along the way.

For more information and a map of the Byway, visit http://coloradobyways.colorado.edu.

Utah!
SCENIC Backways

IN THE NEXT 26 PAGES each of Utah's **Backways** is described with route descriptions and photographs. Backways are grouped together, sharing a map and showing you their proximity to each other.

These roads are designated "Backways" rather than "Byways" for one primary reason – safety. These roads generally do not meet full federal safety standards, meaning they are not wide enough, or graded enough, or level enough to be safe year-round, for passenger cars. They do, however, meet our highest standard of scenic, recreational and historical criteria, and we share them with you.

Utah! Scenic Backways pass through some of the most enthusiastically beautiful country in the world – mountain streams, stands of maples and Douglas fir, red rock spires and extraordinary panoramas. These roads lead to incredible adventures – camping, rock climbing, wildlife viewing, fishing – and solitude is not a promise, but a real possibility.

This section of the book comes with a serious warning. These roads vary widely in their degrees of difficulty. **Backway** travel is an adventure to be taken seriously. Some are narrow, some are easily traveled in good weather but impassable in wet or winter conditions, some are downright dangerous for the unprepared traveler. Some cross isolated, unpredictable terrain. Plan to be self-sufficient, with water (in summer, a gallon per person per day), food, a spare tire, protection from weather, and camping supplies. Ask locally for road and weather conditions. There is a listing of local BLM and Forest Service offices in the back of this book.

Please! Take extra care when planning your Backway drive. All travelers, regardless of where they are going, should have a good road map. The maps in this book are not intended to be the visitor's sole source of information. Detailed maps may be obtained through the **Bureau of Land Management**, **Forest Service**, **Utah Travel Council** or the **U.S. Geological Survey**. At the very least, all travelers should have a **Utah Department of Transportation official highway map**.

Large Photo: Mojave Desert/Joshua Tree Road Backway, No. 58 (pg 84) — Mel Lewis

Top Photo: Grosvenor Arch, Cottonwood Canyon Road Backway, No. 49 (pg 82) — F. Jensen

Bottom Photo: Deep Creek Mountains Backway No. 21 (pg 72) — Tom Till

Utah!
SCENIC Backways

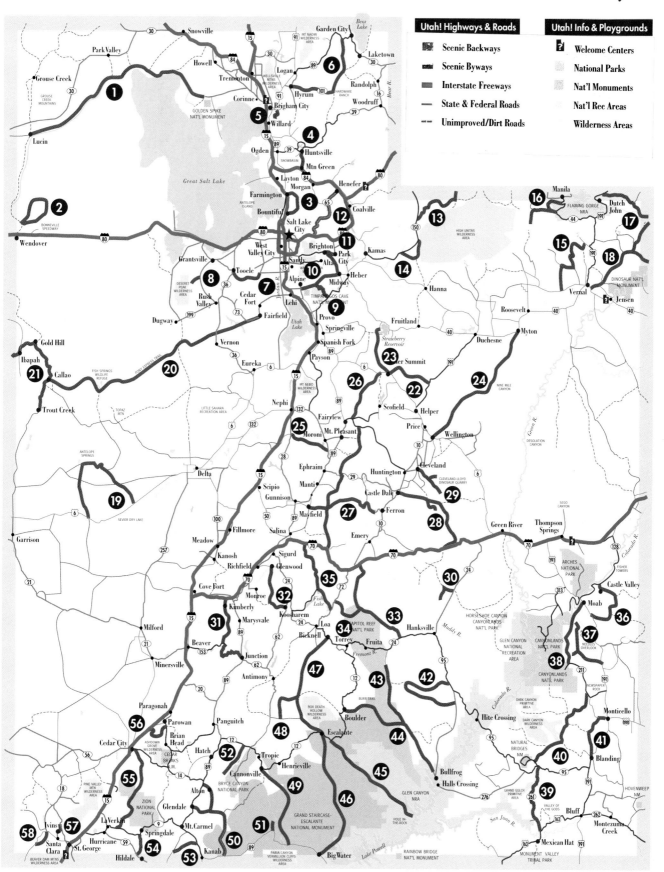

❶ CENTRAL PACIFIC RAILROAD TRAIL

Traveling This Backway: Begin at Locomotive Springs National Waterfowl Management Area located 18 miles south of the town of Snowville. From there, the road travels across the BLM managed desert following the abandoned Central Pacific Railroad grade through the old town sites of Kelton, Terrace and Watercress to Lucin and the Utah/Nevada border. The route is approximately 80 miles one way. Plan on at least three hours travel time.

Road Conditions: This road is graded gravel and dirt. Approximately half of it is maintained as a country road. The remaining portion is not

maintained. Only four-wheel drive vehicles should attempt to follow the railroad grade through the Peplin Mountains. There are no vehicle restrictions on the rest of the railroad grade, but four-wheel drive vehicles with chains, and towrope or winch are recommended, particularly during wet weather conditions. This is an isolated area. Care must be taken to have adequate food, water, first aid supplies, gasoline and spare tires. The Backway is open year-round, but it is suggested that travel be attempted in dry, mild weather.

Scenery and Attractions: Rolling hills and flat lands make up the terrain of this area. Crossing the northern extension of the Great Salt Lake Desert, this "trail" showcases the northern rim of the Great Salt Lake Depression. The route represents miles of the original railroad grade which have lain unaltered since 1903, and upon inspection remain in remarkable condition today. The solitude of the desert and the remnants of Utah's railroad history are the prominent features of the Backway.

❷ SILVER ISLAND MOUNTAIN LOOP

Traveling This Backway: Exit I-80 at Exit #2 just east of Wendover. Heading north toward the salt flat desert east of Wendover, Utah, (half of Wendover is in Nevada) this Backway circles BLM's solitary Silver Island Mountains. The loop is 54 miles long. Two and one-half to three hours travel time is recommended.

Road Conditions: This is a graded gravel and dirt road that is maintained on an "as needed" schedule. It may be traveled in any type of vehicle, however a four-wheel drive is recommended and is necessary to explore any of the rocky canyons, washes or gullies of the range. Open year-round, this Backway is safer and more passable in the dry months of summer and fall.

Scenery and Attractions: Opportunities for hiking, camping, photography, rock collecting and sightseeing are all accessed via this route. The loop also provides the chance to explore historic trails including the wagon ruts of pioneer caravans from 135 years ago. The Silver Island Mountains are rugged and rocky. They are surrounded by the remnants of ancient Lake Bonneville, evidenced by the encircling miles of silver-white mud and salt. A unique feature of this loop is that often views appear distorted, with distances running together or becoming disguised in the heat, reflection, or curvature of the earth.

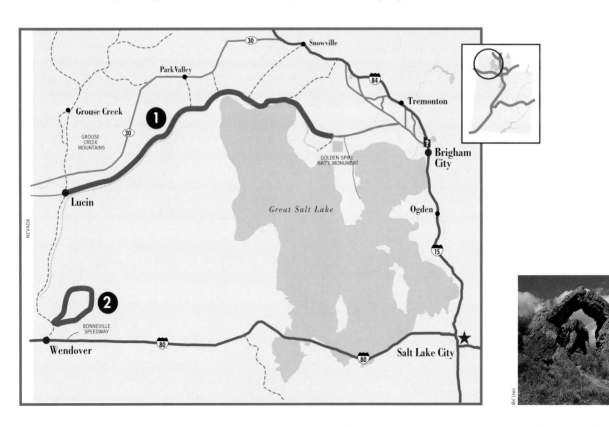

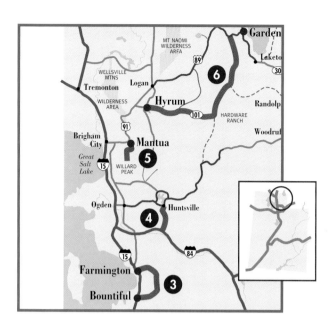

❸ BOUNTIFUL / FARMINGTON LOOP

Traveling This Backway: The Bountiful/Farmington Loop is comprised of three Wasatch-Cache National Forest roads. The route begins in Bountiful and is accessed by traveling east on 400 North to 1300 East – and then turning north onto the Ward Canyon Road. This Backway is 24 miles long and ends in Farmington. Travel time is about two and one-half hours.

Road Conditions: The loop is a gravel road, which is often rough and washboarded. Road grades climbing the mountainsides are steep. Passenger cars can generally travel the road during good weather, but prepare to drive slowly and stop to make way for oncoming traffic. This Backway is closed in the winter.

Scenery and Attractions: This route is best known for its scenic views. Vistas of the Great Salt Lake are stunning. From Francis and Bountiful peaks, the mountain ranges of the west desert are clearly defined. Vegetation is mostly scrub brush, but stands of pine and fir are sprinkled throughout the route.

❹ TRAPPERS LOOP ROAD

Traveling This Backway: This Backway follows SR-167 and begins in the town of Mountain Green. It continues to Huntsville on SR-39. The Trappers Loop is nine miles long and requires less than 20 minutes travel time.

Road Conditions: The road is paved with two travel lanes and passing lanes on up-hill stretches. Portions of the loop have a steep grade. The route is open year-round and easily traveled in passenger vehicles.

Scenery and Attractions: Flanked by rolling hills covered in brush and aspen, this Backway provides splendid views of the backside of Mt. Ogden and of Snowbasin Ski Resort and Strawberry Bowl. Surrounding mountain peaks add interest, and wildlife watching opportunities abound. Trappers Loop is a major point of access to Ogden area ski resorts and summer recreation favorites.

❺ WILLARD PEAK ROAD

Traveling This Backway: This Backway heads south from Mantua to Willard Basin, then climbs to Inspiration Point near Willard Peak. It is a 14-mile drive that ascends from 4,200 feet at Mantua to 9,400 feet at Inspiration Point in the Wasatch-Cache National Forest. Plan at least one and one-half hours travel time each way.

Road Conditions: The Willard Peak Road is dirt surface with some gravel stretches. It is slippery when wet. Because of occasional gullies, high clearance vehicles are recommended. The narrow road is generally closed by snow in late October, remaining closed until June.

Scenery and Attractions: This Backway winds through forests of aspen, spruce and fir and is colorful in any season. You will see evidence of terracing done by the Civilian Conservation Corps in the 1930s to prevent flooding. Perry Reservoir, about half way, is an excellent rest stop. A sweeping view of the Great Salt Lake is found at Inspiration Point.

❻ HARDWARE RANCH ROAD

Traveling This Backway: Beginning on SR-101, three miles east of Hyrum, the road travels Blacksmith Fork Canyon to Hardware Ranch. It then moves steadily north through the Wasatch-Cache National Forest to US-89, ten miles west of Bear Lake. The Backway is approximately 25 miles long. Plan one to two hours travel time.

Road Conditions: The first 18 miles of this route, to Hardware Ranch, are asphalt and maintained year-round. Other portions are single lane dirt road with infrequent turnouts. These sections become impassable during wet weather. In winter, the portion of the Backway from Hardware Ranch to the Sinks is closed and becomes a popular, groomed snowmobile trail.

Scenery and Attractions: Blacksmith Fork Canyon displays vivid fall foliage. The steep canyon walls and cliffs provide interest year-round. Elk wintering at Hardware Ranch are a popular attraction. Sinkholes found later in the drive at Middle Sinks are the result of eons of erosion caused by water seepage. Because of the unique drainage and trapping of winter air, the lowest temperature ever recorded in the lower 48 states was in Middle Sinks. This Backway is forested and is particularly popular in the summer and fall. Wildlife is plentiful and there is a spectacular view of Bear Lake near the road's end. Limber Pine Trail, a self-guided nature trail, is found a quarter-mile east of the terminus.

7 MIDDLE CANYON ROAD

Traveling This Backway: Traveling south from Tooele this Backway follows Vine Street east, leading straight up Middle Canyon then over Butterfield Pass to the town of Lark. A side spur accesses the Kennecott Copper Mine Overlook. The route directly to Lark is about 15 miles long and requires under an hour's drive time. The side trip to the mine overlook makes this a 25-mile Backway and adds at least a half-hour to the travel time.

Road Conditions: The majority of this road, on the west side of Butterfield pass, is paved. On the eastern side, the road is dirt and generally washboarded. This route is generally steep and portions have narrow switchbacks. A four-wheel drive or high clearance vehicle is recommended. This Backway is dangerous during inclement weather and is closed in the winter.

Scenery and Attractions: Climbing to Butterfield Pass, the beauty of the Oquirrh Mountains is unparalleled. From the summit and the Kennecott Overlook, excellent views of the Wasatch Mountains, the Salt Lake Valley, Utah Lake, Kennecott Copper Mine, the Stansbury Mountains, and the vast Great Salt Lake provide a varied panorama.

8 SOUTH WILLOW ROAD

Traveling This Backway: The South Willow Road originates six miles south of Grantsville and winds west through the Wasatch-Cache National Forest for approximately eight miles to Deseret Peak. Travel time is approximately one-half hour.

Road Conditions: The first half of this Backway is paved road, the second half is gravel and natural rock surface. The road is rough and steep, but acceptable for passenger cars if driven slowly. Maintenance is sporadic. Ask locally about weather and road conditions before traveling this route. This Backway is closed during the winter.

Scenery and Attractions: This road is the primary access to the west side of the Stansbury Mountains and the hiking trails in the Deseret Peak Wilderness. Vegetation begins with sagebrush and juniper and as the Backway climbs, changes to Douglas fir and aspen. The route features several narrows, where rock cliffs tower on either side with barely enough room to allow passage of the roadway.

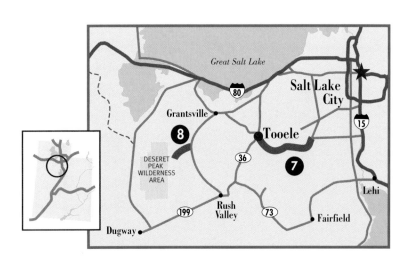

ALPINE SCENIC LOOP

Traveling This Backway: The Uinta National Forest's Alpine Scenic Loop begins at the mouth of American Fork Canyon on SR-92 at 5,000 feet, and follows the canyon to its crest at 8,000 feet. From the summit, the road winds down toward Provo Canyon and US-189. This Backway is 24 miles long. Plan one hour for travel time.

Road Conditions: The Alpine Loop is a paved, two lane road. Because of the steep grade and narrow curves, pulling trailers is prohibited. The road is closed in the winter due to snow, but is available for snowmobile travel.

Scenery and Attractions: Lush vegetation characterizes this route. At the summit of American Fork Canyon, vistas of Mt. Timpanogos are visible through impressive aspen groves. Campgrounds and picnic areas are numerous. This Loop also provides access to Timpanogos Cave National Monument and Robert Redford's Sundance Ski and Summer Resort. Trails lead from the road into the Mt. Timpanogos and Lone Peak Wilderness Areas. This Backway is a particularly popular autumn drive.

⑩ CASCADE SPRINGS

Traveling This Backway: This Backway begins on the Alpine Loop at the summit between American Fork and Provo Canyons. The road travels to Cascade Springs in the Uinta National Forest, then north to Wasatch Mountain State Park. This Backway is approximately 25 miles and requires one hour for travel time. Plan extra time to stop at Cascade Springs.

Road Conditions: The first portion of this route is a two lane paved road leading to Cascade Springs. The remaining route has a well-graded, dirt surface. High clearance vehicles are recommended, but when dry, the route may be traveled with care in a passenger car. This road is closed in winter.

Scenery and Attractions: Beginning in the aspen groves of the Alpine Loop, views from the road include Mt. Timpanogos, the Wasatch Mountains and the distant High Uintas. Cascade Springs features large springs cascading down the mountain slope in a series of limestone terraces and pools. The sight has barrier-free access and interpretive information. At the Backway's end, Wasatch Mountain State Park is popular for year-round recreation.

⑪ GUARDSMAN PASS ROAD

Traveling This Backway: The Guardsman Pass Backway follows SR-224 beginning in Wasatch Mountain State Park. From the visitor center, it takes the north fork of the road past the campground and golf course heading toward Park City. Mid-route, the road reaches the Brighton/Park City Junction in the Wasatch-Cache National Forest. The Backway route provides two options. The Brighton cut-off travels over the mountain to Brighton Resort in Big Cottonwood Canyon. This route is just over 14 miles and requires 45 minutes. The Park City cut-off heads down to the mountain ski resort community of Park City. The route is just over 22 miles and requires one hour.

Road Conditions: This is a partially paved, graded road with rocky surface in some areas. Expect washboard conditions and steep grades at several points. In dry weather, the road is safe for passenger cars. The section from Park City Junction to Brighton should not be attempted in wet weather. The entire Guardsman Pass Backway is closed in the winter.

Scenery and Attractions: Mountain panoramas and valleys highlight this Backway. From the summit of Guardsman Pass, the forested Heber Valley spreads beneath the road, and to the east are views of the High Uintas Wilderness. To the west is Big Cottonwood Canyon and views of the Oquirrh and Stansbury Mountains.

PIONEER MEMORIAL BACKWAY

Traveling This Backway: From Salt Lake's Hogle Zoo on Sunnyside Avenue, this Backway leads directly into Emigration Canyon. Following the canyon, the route turns northeast into East Canyon on SR-65 and on to the town of Henefer. This Backway is 34 miles. Allow an hour and a half drive time each way. Alternate routes back to Salt Lake are available, such as I-80 past Park City or I-84 through Ogden.

Road Conditions: The entire distance from Salt Lake City to Henefer is paved and has a moderate grade. The road is closed in the winter.

Scenery and Attractions: This Backway follows the route used by the Donner-Reed Expedition in 1846. In 1847 the first party of Mormon pioneers to arrive in the Salt Lake Valley used the route, and it soon became established as a major frontier route for Mormons and other traveling parties. Historical markers dot the drive. This road also accesses East Canyon State Park and is a popular fall foliage drive.

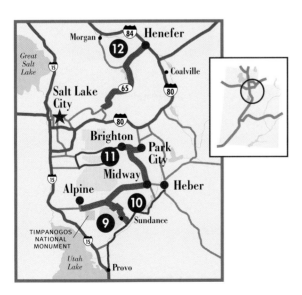

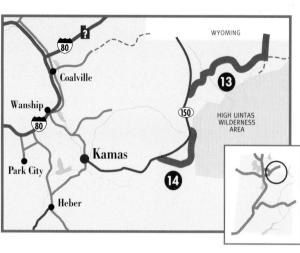

⑬ NORTH SLOPE ROAD

Traveling This Backway: From six miles south of the Utah/Wyoming border on SR-150, this Backway runs east past the China Meadows/China Lake area of the Wasatch-Cache National Forest before turning north to Stateline Reservoir. The road is 38 miles long and requires two and one-half hours travel time, partially because of elevation changes.

Road Conditions: This dirt and gravel road contains single and double lane sections. Use extreme caution in rainy weather. Heavy snow closes the road in winter.

Scenery and Attractions: As the Backway climbs and descends this mountainous area, it winds through stands of lodgepole pine mixed with aspen, spruce and fir. The variety of forest growth makes this a particularly attractive autumn drive. Remnants of logging operations dot the route. The road offers plenty of opportunity to view the surrounding peaks of the Uinta Mountains. Camping, fishing, and wildlife viewing is plentiful. From the dam at Stateline Reservoir, you will see a stunning view of the High Uintas Wilderness, including 13,528-foot King's Peak, the highest point in the state.

⑭ BROADHEAD MEADOW ROAD

Traveling This Backway: To travel the Broadhead Meadow Road across the Wasatch-Cache National Forest, turn onto the Murdock Basin Road, accessed from SR-150, 24 miles east of Kamas. From a signed intersection the Broadhead Meadow Road circles to join SR-150 just south of the Upper Provo River Falls. The loop is approximately four and one-half miles, and requires one hour of driving time.

Road Conditions: This road is unsurfaced and has a rocky bed. High clearance vehicles are necessary, and four-wheel drive is needed in some areas. In winter SR-150 is closed, blocking access to the Backway.

Scenery and Attractions: This road winds through lodgepole pine forests. Scenic points include views of surrounding peaks towering to 11,000 feet. Broadhead Meadow, adjacent to the road, is a large alpine meadow with a lovely creek, and is a popular fishing spot. Near the beginning of the route the scar of a 1980 fire provides the opportunity to see a new forest beginning amidst total forest destruction.

15 RED CLOUD/DRY FORK LOOP

Traveling This Backway: This Backway begins at the border of the Ashley National Forest, accessed from US-191, 14 miles north of Vernal. It then runs west and south to Dry Fork. The route is about 45 miles long and driving time is two hours.

Road Conditions: Portions of this Backway are paved or gravel. However, about half of the route is on dirt roads, which are rough and not recommended when wet. The higher elevations are snow-covered from late fall to mid-spring. During the winter, the entire route is generally closed by snow.

Scenery and Attractions: This is a scenic drive in the beautiful Uinta Mountains. It travels through aspen groves, open meadows and forests of lodgepole pine. A variety of large and small wildlife may be sighted. There are numerous streams, popular for fishing. Views of towering mountains highlight the route. In the lower portion of Dry Fork Canyon, remnants of early settlements are framed by sandstone cliffs.

16 SHEEP CREEK/SPIRIT LAKE LOOP

Traveling This Backway: This Backway consists of the Sheep Creek Loop and the Spirit Lake Road in the Ashley National Forest. It begins on Sheep Creek Loop, 15 miles west of the US-191/SR-44 junction. The Sheep Creek Loop is a 13-mile road that returns to SR-44, five miles south of Manila. The Spirit Lake Road is a spur route off the Sheep Creek Loop with a 17-mile travel distance to Spirit Lake. Returning from Spirit Lake requires back-tracking to the Sheep Creek Loop. Total driving distance for the loop and the spur, including the return trip from Spirit Lake, is 48 miles and requires two and one-half hours travel time.

Frank Jensen

Road Conditions: The main canyon loop is partially paved, with stretches of gravel and dirt road. Off the main canyon road, the road to Spirit Lake is gravel surface. Although it is graded in the spring, the road is usually wash-boarded by late summer. This Backway may be traveled by passenger car. Use extra caution on the Spirit Lake road. Snow closes the route from late fall to early spring.

Scenery and Attractions: The scenery along this Backway is varied. It ranges from pine and aspen forest and flower-filled meadows surrounding Spirit Lake to the towering rock spires of Sheep Creek Canyon. The visually dramatic Uinta Fault, which runs for more than 100 miles along the north slope of the Uinta Mountains, is clearly distinguished along this road. Viewpoints of Sheep Creek Bay on Flaming Gorge are found off the Backway on SR-44.

17 JONES HOLE ROAD

Traveling This Backway: Four miles east of Vernal, on SR-149, this Backway leaves the Ashley Valley climbing north 2,600 feet to Diamond Mountain Plateau. From there it turns east and drops to Jones Hole National Fish Hatchery. The route is 80 miles round-trip and takes at least two hours to drive. Allow extra time for sightseeing or to follow the mile hike from the Hatchery to the Green River in Dinosaur National Monument.

Road Conditions: This Backway is entirely paved and has two lanes. However, it is narrow and has narrow shoulders. The higher elevation portions of the route may be impassable in winter.

Scenery and Attractions: Early in the route, the road crosses a bench of Mancos Shale. The ascent of Diamond Mountain is flanked by sagebrush and grasses, and aspen and pine are found on the higher slopes. Deer and elk inhabit the area. The road to Jones Hole drops dramatically into a narrow, rugged canyon. The Jones Hole Hatchery produces trout for streams, lakes and reservoirs in Utah, Wyoming and Colorado.

18 BROWN'S PARK ROAD

Traveling This Backway: The Brown's Park Road departs from the Diamond Mountain Plateau on the Jones Hole Road Scenic Backway. It travels north across Diamond Mountain then down Crouse Canyon entering Brown's Park. The route continues into Colorado crossing the Green River via a suspension bridge, which accommodates only one vehicle at a time. After crossing the bridge the road turns west re-entering Utah. A short side trip visits BLM's John Jarvie Historic Site, a preserved remnant of the frontier west. The Backway passes through narrow, winding Jessie Ewing Canyon then onto its end at US-191, five miles north of Dutch John. This drive is approximately 50 miles and requires two hours travel time.

Road Conditions: After leaving the paved Jones Hole Road, the Backway is a graded dirt road acceptable in good weather for passenger cars. The road is closed in the winter and should not be traveled during heavy rain.

Scenery and Attractions: The Brown's Park area harbored outlaws as well as settlers. Both Crouse and Jessie Ewing Canyons were named for early residents. Crouse Canyon is particularly stunning as the road passes through vertical cliffs flanked by pinyon and juniper-covered side hills. Brown's Park once housed a trading post operated by Jim Bridger. Elk, antelope and mule deer are common in the area.

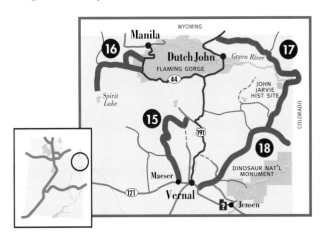

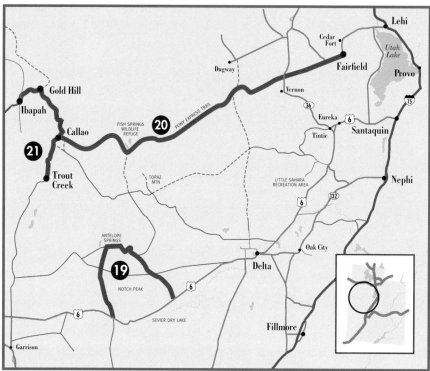

20 PONY EXPRESS TRAIL

Traveling This Backway: To follow the Pony Express Trail, head west from the town of Fairfield (located west of Utah Lake) through Faust, over Lookout Summit, and past Simpson Springs and Fish Springs. The road then travels through the Snake Valley to Callao and northwest to Ibapah. There are no services along this 133-mile Backway. Allow five to six hours travel time with interpretive stops.

Road Conditions: The first five miles and the last two miles of this "trail" are asphalt. In between lie 126 miles of maintained gravel and dirt road. The route is open throughout the year, however, the best and safest seasons are spring and fall. There are no vehicle restrictions, but four-wheel drive vehicles with chains, tow-rope or winch are recommended after heavy rain or snow.

Scenery and Attractions: The Pony Express Trail is marked with the monuments or ruins of 14 Pony Express Station sites. This Backway crosses desert valleys, climbs remote mountain passes and serves as the main street of small, isolated communities. A popular stop is Fish Springs, the most remote wildlife refuge in the continental United States.

19 NOTCH PEAK LOOP

Traveling This Backway: The Notch Peak Loop is accessed by traveling 43 miles west of Delta on US-6/50. From this point the 50-mile loop circles north through BLM public land around the peaks in the rugged House Range Mountains to Dome Canyon Pass, through the pass, and then south around the western side of the range and back to US-50. Allow at least two hours to travel this loop.

Road Conditions: This Backway is a maintained gravel road. It is accessible by passenger cars except during snow or flash floods. During some winters, the Dome Canyon Pass section is closed from December to February due to snow accumulation.

Scenery and Attractions: The mountains of the House Range feature exposed sedimentary rock layers of ancient origin. This is particularly pronounced on the western wall of the range. Notch Peak is said to be the largest limestone formation in the state. Towering to 9,700 feet, its ragged silhouette dominates the desert skyline. To the north the area surrounding Swasey Peak harbors well-preserved trilobites and other fossil specimens.

21 DEEP CREEK MOUNTAINS

Traveling This Backway: A side trip off the Pony Express Trail, this Backway begins in Callao and leads to five canyons in the Deep Creek Range before its conclusion in Trout Creek. It is approximately 15 miles from Callao to Trout Creek. Driving into the five canyons adds an extra 10 to 15 miles. Travel time varies with the amount of exploration planned.

Road Conditions: This Backway is gravel surfaced. It has seasonal closures from late November to April because of snow accumulation. Four-wheel drive is recommended for travel into all canyons along this route because roads are steep and rocky.

Scenery and Attractions: The Deep Creek Mountains represent a fault formation mountain range. The highest point, Haystack Peak, rises 8,000 feet above the desert to an elevation of 12,101 feet. The rugged peaks harbor no maintained trails. Mule deer, elk, mountain lions and big horn sheep live among the varied terrain, which ranges from salt desert shrubs to firs near the timberline.

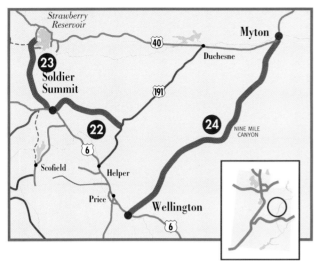

22 RESERVATION RIDGE

Traveling This Backway: This route begins near Soldier Summit on US-6. It ends at the junction with US-191 between the road following the eastern direction of the White River's right fork while climbing through the Uinta and Ashley National Forests to an 8,900-foot ridge. The road is approximately 45 miles long and requires two hours driving time.

Road Conditions: This Backway is a single lane dirt road. It is closed from November 15 to May 15 due to weather and road surface conditions. Four-wheel drive is required when the road is wet and is recommended year-round on portions of the road on top of the Ridge.

Scenery and Attractions: From the top of the ridge, views of the Strawberry River and its drainages are visible in all directions. Stands of aspen and pine provide color and variety to the landscape. Plateaus and steep canyons add to this scenic variety. Cliffs and ledges located at the breaks of the plateaus form colorful geologic features.

23 WHITE RIVER/STRAWBERRY ROAD

Traveling This Backway: Beginning on US-6 at 7,500-foot Soldier Summit, this Backway follows the left fork of the White River in the Uinta National Forest. The road ascends to the head of Willow Creek at 8,800 feet, then leads down Racetrack Canyon and Trail Hollow. It joins the Indian Creek Road at Strawberry Reservoir then runs north to US-40, 23 miles east of Heber.

Road Conditions: Road type varies from dirt and single lane gravel surface to two lanes, improved gravel and paved all-weather road. High clearance vehicles are recommended on the dirt portions. The road is closed by snow and surface conditions from November 15 to May 15. In good weather, travel time is approximately one hour.

Scenery and Attractions: The views along this Backway are of aspen and pine forests, and open fields of sage and grass. Wildlife viewing is rewarding. The route also provides access to beautiful forest backcountry and numerous side trips. Strawberry Reservoir offers camping, fishing and picnic facilities.

24 NINE MILE CANYON

Traveling This Backway: The turn-off to Nine Mile Canyon is approximately two miles east of Wellington on US-191. The Backway is 78-miles long (not nine miles!) and ends at the junction of US-40 one mile west of Myton. Allow three hours travel time. In addition to the main route, side roads lead into several other canyons and onto the West Tavaputs Plateau.

Road Conditions: This route is a double lane, graded gravel and dirt surface road. The initial portion near Wellington is paved. The road can be driven in passenger cars during good weather. Several normally dry wash crossings in the canyon may be obstacles to travel after heavy rain. Four-wheel drive is recommended for traveling side roads. This route should not be driven in vehicles longer than 22 feet.

Scenery and Attractions: Nine Mile Canyon is known as a major representative area of the prehistoric Fremont Culture. The canyon houses myriad rock art panels along the main road and in side canyons. Petroglyphs (carvings on rock faces) and pictographs (paintings on rock faces) depict animals, hunting scenes and iconic figures. Careful observers may spot cliff granaries on high canyon ledges. In the 1800s, the canyon was used by both fur trappers and the army. Iron telegraph poles, stage stations and settler cabins are common sights. Vegetation and terrain along this Backway vary from high desert species to aspen groves. The buff colored cliffs of the canyon are highlighted by balanced rocks and window arches. Deer and elk are seen frequently.

25 CHICKEN CREEK ROAD

Traveling This Backway: Beginning in the town of Levan, the Chicken Creek Road heads east, bending south just out of town. The Backway proceeds east through the Uinta National Forest and up and over the San Pitch Mountains. It continues down Wales Canyon and on to the community of Chester in Sanpete Valley. Total mileage is about 16 miles and it takes just over an hour for the complete trip.

Road Conditions: The Backway is graveled from Levan to Chicken Creek Campground, a distance of five miles. From the campground east to the community of Wales, road surface is dirt and conditions require the use of four-wheel drive vehicles. This segment of the road is closed during the winter months. The road is paved from the community of Wales to Chester and US-89.

Scenery and Attractions: From Levan, the Backway passes through mountain brush, pinyon, juniper and oak on its way to the ridge top of the San Pitch Mountain range. At 8,200 feet, the Backway reaches the crest of the mountains and large open grassy areas fill the vista. As the road descends to the Sanpete Valley floor, spectacular view points are available of the Wasatch Plateau and associated canyons on the eastern side of the Sanpete Valley. Gray and red shale and sandstone rock outcrops are prominent along the drive, providing scenic contrast to mosaic vegetation with aspen clumps and pockets of conifers.

26 SKYLINE DRIVE

Traveling This Backway: Accessed from US-6, 18-miles east of Thistle at the Tucker Rest Area, this Backway follows the left fork of Clear Creek then moves south toward I-70 and on to Taylor Flat eighteen miles east of Salina. The route is 87-miles long and traverses through the Manti-La Sal and toward Fishlake National Forests at elevations near 10,900 feet.

Road Conditions: Portions of this Backway are passable by two-wheel drive vehicles year-round. Other sections are recommended only for high clearance vehicles during dry conditions. Four-wheel drive may be necessary on some portions of the road. To ensure a safe trip, contact a local Manti-La Sal Forest ranger for information on travel conditions.

Scenery and Attractions: Scenery along road way includes views of the Oquirrh Mountains, Mt. Nebo, distant valleys, the Roan Plateau and an abundance of forested high-mountain settings. Wildlife is abundant in the area, as are recreational opportunities.

Mel Lewis

27 MAYFIELD-FERRON SCENIC BACKWAY

Traveling This Backway: To travel this Backway, begin in the town of Mayfield (accessed via SR-137). This 50-mile route climbs from 5,500 feet at its origin to join the Skyline Drive at 10,700 feet in the Manti-La Sal National Forest. After crossing the Skyline Drive, Ferron Reservoir marks the road's descent. The Backway terminates in Ferron at an elevation of 5,900 feet.

Road Conditions: In good weather it is possible to travel this graded gravel road in a passenger car. The route is closed during the winter.

Scenery and Attractions: The mountain environment of this Backway offers several reservoirs and camping areas. The vegetation includes stands of pinyon and juniper as well as aspen clustered forests and high mountain meadows.

Tom Till

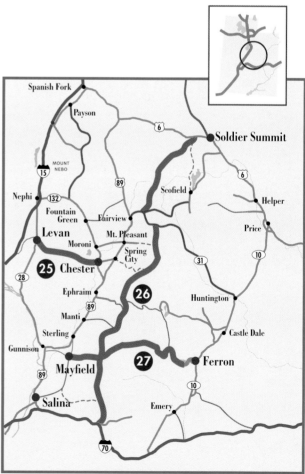

28 WEDGE OVERLOOK / BUCKHORN DRAW

Traveling This Backway: The 20-mile section of this Backway leading to BLM's Wedge Overlook begins by driving north from Castle Dale on SR-10 for one mile, then east on a gravel road for 13 miles. The road turns south at a signed intersection following the left fork for six miles to the Wedge Overlook. Vantage points along the rim provide canyon views – each different from the next. To travel the Buckhorn Draw portion of the Backway, return six miles to the signed intersection and turn right toward the head of Buckhorn Draw. This route continues through the draw and across the San Rafael River on a swinging bridge. The Backway ends at ranch exit #129 on I-70. The Buckhorn Draw section to I-70 is approximately 25 miles. Allow 45 minutes travel time between Castle Dale and the Wedge Overlook. Allow one hour travel time for the Buckhorn Draw/I-70 portion of the Backway.

Road Conditions: After leaving paved highway SR-10, this graveled Backway is graded regularly and is passable for two-wheel drive vehicles in good weather. The road is occasionally impassable during winter months due to snow or wet conditions.

Scenery and Attractions: The road to the Wedge Overlook climbs through rolling pinyon and juniper woodland until it ends suddenly at the edge of the Wedge Overlook, sometimes called "Utah's Little Grand Canyon." Over 1,200 feet below, the San Rafael River winds its way between the canyon walls. The Buckhorn Draw portion of the Backway follows a narrow, winding sandstone canyon. South of the San Rafael River, the Backway travels through open range lands and pinyon-juniper terrain to I-70.

Frank Jensen

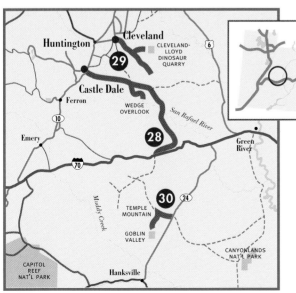

29 DINOSAUR QUARRY / CEDAR OVERLOOK

Traveling This Backway: Embarking from the town of Cleveland, this Backway proceeds east following signs through scenic badlands to the desert oasis of Desert Lake Waterfowl Management Area. The road then turns south and continues to BLM's Cleveland-Lloyd Dinosaur Quarry. From the quarry it is necessary to back-track six miles to a "T" intersection before proceeding south to the Cedar Mountain Overlook also on BLM public land.

Road Conditions: The road surface of this 39-mile Backway is not paved. It is generally smooth and passable in good weather for two-wheel drive vehicles. The road gets muddy during wet conditions and should be avoided. Two hours, each way, are needed to travel this route.

Scenery and Attractions: The hills running along the Backway are striped with pink, gray and purple rock, and illustrate the dinosaur-bone bearing Morrison Formation. The Cleveland-Lloyd Quarry has produced more complete dinosaur skeletons than any other site in the world. The quarry visitor center and viewing areas are open from Easter through Labor Day. Call the BLM in Price at (435) 637-4584 for opening hours and days of operation. The portion of the route ascending Cedar Mountain rises almost 2,000 feet, changing from desert to woodland terrain. The Cedar Mountain Recreation area has restrooms, picnic facilities, a nature trail, panoramic views of the San Rafael Swell, and geologic interpretive exhibits.

30 TEMPLE MOUNTAIN / GOBLIN VALLEY ROAD

Traveling This Backway: Twenty four miles south of I-70 on SR-24 is the Temple Mountain Junction, the origin of this Backway. From here, a paved road travels west to Temple Mountain. At a signed junction the Backway turns south to Goblin Valley State Park on an oiled road. The Backway is about 15 miles long and requires one hour without stops.

Road Conditions: This route is a paved and oiled road.

Scenery and Attractions: The view along the route is dominated by the San Rafael Reef, which rises abruptly to dissect the surrounding desert. Temple Mountain, named for its resemblance to the Salt Lake Mormon Temple, is the highest point along the reef. The mountain was the sight of extensive uranium mining during the 1950s. To the south, the Henry Mountains rise above lower buttes. At Goblin Valley State Park an entrance fee is charged. Here, hundreds of oddly shaped red sandstone "goblins" invite closer examination. A campground and modern facilities are available.

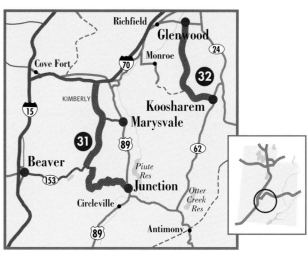

31 KIMBERLY/BIG JOHN ROAD

Traveling This Backway: The route begins at the city of Junction on US-89. Turning onto SR-153, it continues past Puffer Lake and Elk Meadows. On a Fishlake National Forest road, the Backway turns north to Big John Flat and climbs over the Tushar Mountains. The route continues through the historic Kimberly mining district to the freeway interchange near Fremont Indian State Park at I-70. The road is about 40 miles long, with a travel time of three hours. One point in the Backway also provides access to the Kent's Lake Loop. The spur route leaves the junction of SR-153, traveling southwest about 11 miles to rejoin SR-153 in Beaver Canyon. This loop provides access to LeBaron Reservoir, Anderson Meadow Reservoir, Kent's Lake and Little Reservoir.

Road Conditions: The Kimberly/Big John Road is generally suitable for travel in a passenger car, however there are some narrow, rough areas and some extreme grades, and high clearance vehicles are recommended. The road surface is dirt and becomes slick when wet. The route is closed in the winter and spring. Travel trailers are not recommended.

Scenery and Attractions: This Backway climbs through the Tushar Mountain Range. A series of high mountain meadows punctuate the route. In late summer, wildflowers are found growing between fields of lava rock and on the tundra. This route has elevations ranging from 6,000 to 11,000 feet and spectacular views of mountain peaks as high as 12,139 feet. Sighting animals, particularly large mule deer, is common along this Backway. Fall colors make this drive an autumn favorite.

32 COVE MOUNTAIN ROAD

Traveling This Backway: The Cove Mountain Road in the Fishlake National Forest extends from Koosharem on SR-62, north to Glenwood on SR-119. It is approximately 25 miles long, and drive time is two hours.

Road Conditions: The road surface is graded dirt. This route is acceptable for two-wheel drive vehicles during dry weather. Winter snows close the Backway.

Scenery and Attractions: This route crosses Cove Mountain and extends through the Fishlake National Forest. Summer travel offers cool greenery and wildflowers. The route is particularly popular because of its spectacular autumn scenery and panoramic views of the Sevier and Koosharem Valleys. A favorite stop is the Koosharem Guard Station, one of Utah's first Forest Service buildings, built in 1910.

Steve Greenwood

33 CATHEDRAL VALLEY ROAD

Traveling This Backway: One-half mile west of Cainville on SR-24 this Backway heads north across Cathedral Valley into Capitol Reef National Park, then on to Fremont Junction on I-70. The route is approximately 56 miles long. Three to four hours travel time should be allowed.

Road Conditions: This is a maintained dirt road. Travel is not recommended when the road is wet due to wash crossings and clay soils that become extremely slippery. High clearance vehicles are advised. Portions of the road may be extremely dusty during dry summers. Check locally for weather and road conditions.

Scenery and Attractions: At its beginning, the Backway follows the Cainville Wash. As the road begins to ascend from the wash valley, you will see a panorama of deep maze-like canyons, softly painted hills, and oddly tilted, (up thrust) rock formations. Continuing through the desert, the road enters a corner of Capitol Reef National Park and Lower Cathedral Valley. From the Backway a short side road leads to the Temple of the Sun and Temple of the Moon Formations, free-standing buttes which rise steeply from the valley floor. Further west, at Cathedral Valley Junction, the Backway spurs north through the Last Chance Desert, with striking views of Thousand Lake Plateau and Fishlake National Forest to the west, and striated badlands to the east.

Frank Jensen

34 THOUSAND LAKE MOUNTAIN ROAD

Traveling This Backway: From SR-72, five miles north of Fremont, this Backway travels southeast through the Fishlake National Forest to join the Cathedral Valley Scenic Backway. In Capitol Reef National Park, this Backway loops southwest through the park towards the Elkhorn Campground. The route provides access to the campground and continues back to its point of origin at SR-72. This Backway is 35 miles long and requires two hours travel time.

Road Conditions: The road is primarily single lane graded dirt. Four-wheel drive or high clearance vehicles are recommended. Dust on the roads may be extreme during dry summers. This Backway may be impassable during wet weather.

Scenery and Attractions: The Thousand Lake Road provides panoramic views of surrounding mountain ranges. It also travels through the towering formations of Capitol Reef's upper Cathedral Valley and climbs to provide impressive overlooks and vistas of the valley's terrain.

35 GOOSEBERRY/FREMONT ROAD

Traveling This Backway: Beginning two miles north of Fremont on SR-72, this Backway runs approximately 40 miles through the Fishlake National Forest to its end at I-70 in Salina Canyon. Plan one and one-half hour's drive time.

Road Conditions: This road is paved and favorable for passenger vehicles. Due to steep grades and narrow roadway, high clearance vehicles are recommended. This Backway is closed in the winter.

Scenery and Attractions: The forested Gooseberry/Fremont Road provides access to several high mountains meadows and streams. It is also a popular route to the Fishlake Basin. The abundance of trees makes this road a popular fall color trek.

François Camoin

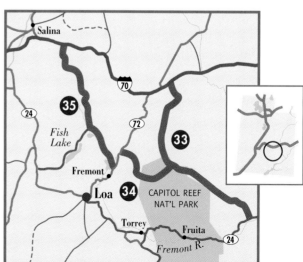

Frank Jensen

 LA SAL MOUNTAIN LOOP ROAD

Traveling This Backway: This Backway begins from US-191 six miles south of Moab. It winds north over the LaSal Mountains in the Manti-La Sal National Forest and through Castle Valley to end at SR-128. The route is sixty miles long and takes two to four hours to complete.

Road Conditions: This road is paved except for a couple of short gravel portions. There are also sections of narrow, steep switchbacks. The La Sal Mountain portion of the road is impassable in winter, due to snow. This Backway is suitable for passenger car traffic. It is not recommended for large RV's or travel trailers.

Scenery and Attractions: This Backway provides scenery ranging from the alpine heights of the La Sal Mountains to the red rock desert of the surrounding Abajo and Henry Mountains. Near the end of the route lies Castle Valley, named for Castle Rock, a tall pinnacle of red sandstone. Also prominent is the Priest and Nuns formation at the opposite end of the ridge. Changes in vegetation are interesting to note as the route proceeds through desert and mountain ecosystems.

37 NEEDLES/ANTICLINE OVERLOOK ROAD

Traveling This Backway: Turning west off US-191, twelve miles south of LaSal Junction, this Backway travels across the desert to access BLM's Needles and Anticline Overlooks. It is a total of 76 miles to visit both overlooks and return to US-191. Allow three to four hours for the tour including stops at viewpoints.

Road Conditions: The first portion of this route is paved. At a "Y" intersection, the paved road to Needles Overlook stems left. The road on the right is gravel and leads to the Anticline Overlook. This Backway is driven year-round, but is closed immediately after severe snowstorms. These roads may be easily traveled in a two-wheel drive vehicle.

Scenery and Attractions: The roads to each overlook offer views of Canyonlands National Park to the west. The alpine backdrop of the La Sal Mountains provides contrast to many colorful sandstone formations along the way. From the Needles Overlook, an expansive view of BLM's Indian Creek Wilderness Study Area and the Needles District of Canyonlands National Park spreads at your feet. The Anticline Overlook is situated on a narrow promontory. Views include the Colorado River, Dead Horse Point State Park, Hurrah Pass and Kane Creek Canyon. Camping is available at Windwhistle and Hatch Point Campgrounds along the Backway.

38 LOCKHART BASIN ROAD

Traveling This Backway: Portions of this Backway are possibly the most challenging four-wheel routes mentioned in this book. This Backway follows Kane Creek Blvd from its intersection with US-191 in Moab to a "Y"intersection with 5th West. The route turns left at this intersection, following a paved road that parallels the Colorado River. The pavement ends at a cattle guard near the entrance to Kane Creek Canyon, and proceeds into the canyon on a gravel road. At a point 10 miles from Moab, the route crosses Kane Creek, an intermittent stream. The creek crossing should not be attempted during high water levels. After crossing the creek, drivers should turn right at a "Y" intersection and begin the climb to Hurrah Pass. At a signed point seven miles from Hurrah Pass, the Backway crosses a wash then veers left joining the Lockhart Basin trail. From here the road travels through a canyon bottom, then climbs a bench. This is the most difficult part of the route and guiding vehicle tracks may disappear following storms. Once out of the canyon, the Backway skirts the base of the adjacent cliffs all the way to SR-211. The distance from Moab to SR-211 is 57 miles. Allow 11 hours travel time. Overnight camping is recommended.

Road Conditions: The paved and gravel road to the Kane Creek ford is suitable for all vehicles. The section from Kane Creek ford to Hurrah Pass is only accessible for high clearance vehicles. A heavy duty, high clearance four-wheel drive vehicle is required from Hurrah Pass south to Lockhart Basin. The rest of the route south to SR-211 may normally be driven with a high clearance vehicle, but may require four-wheel drive. The Backway should be traveled from north to south in order to assess the tough section near the northern end of the Lockhart Basin Trail. The route may be impassable to some vehicles, especially after storm damage, as this steep, narrow and rocky section is rarely maintained. The 20-mile section of trail along the bench north of Lockhart Basin takes six to seven hours to travel because of rocky sections and wash crossings. Travelers on this Backway should be prepared for backcountry travel conditions in a remote area and have extra food, clothing and water for people and vehicles. Consider driving this Backway as a one-way, in-and-out road from SR-211 to Lockhart Basin, to avoid the difficult four-wheel section north of Lockhart Basin.

Scenery and Attractions: The Lockhart Basin Road is a red rock adventure almost entirely on BLM public lands. Views include the Colorado River, serpentine Kane Creek Canyon, Hurrah Pass and the canyon and cliff country adjacent to Canyonlands National Park.

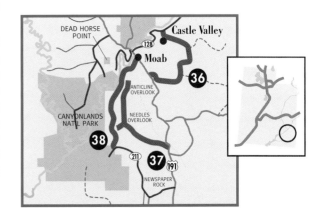

Frank Jensen

Scott Smith

39 TRAIL OF THE ANCIENTS

Traveling This Backway: This is part of an ancient route used by native tribes, which once linked the entire southwest. This Backway follows SR-261, the Moki Dugway, from SR-95 to SR-163. It intersects with SR-316, and travels to its terminus at Goosenecks of the San Juan State Park, overlooking the goosenecks of the San Juan River. The Backway is approximately 37 miles long and travels entirely through BLM public land. It requires one hour travel time.

Road Conditions: The Moki Dugway is a 1,000-foot switchback climb to the top of Cedar Mesa. It includes three miles of gravel road, and the remainder is paved. The Goosenecks of the San Juan spur on SR-316 is also paved. Grades on this route are steep, but passenger vehicles are appropriate year-round. At the top of the Moki Dugway, you can side trip to Muley Point. This graded road is five miles long.

Scenery and Attractions: From the top of the Moki Dugway, panoramic views of Monument Valley and Valley of the Gods present stunning examples of the red rock artistry of this desert country. From the Goosenecks Overlook, a 1,500 foot chasm drops to the meandering San Juan River below. This is one of the most striking examples of entrenched river meanders on the North American continent. The Backway also provides access to BLM's Cedar Mesa Recreation Area which includes Grand Gulch Primitive Area. Travel into the Recreation area, which is rich in remnants of prehistoric Indian culture, is by foot or horseback only. The Kane Gulch Ranger Station, open April to September, provides information on this area. Muley Point Overlook offers spectacular views of Monument Valley to the south and Navajo Mountain to the west.

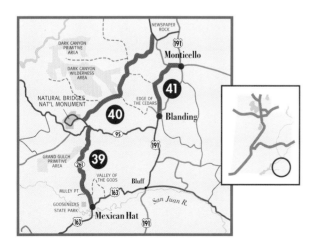

40 ELK RIDGE ROAD

Traveling This Backway: This Scenic Backway begins about 25 miles west of Blanding at the junction of SR-95 and SR-275, which accesses Natural Bridges National Monument. The route leads one mile west on SR-275, then turns on Forest Road 088 ascending through the Bears Ears mountain formation to the spine of Elk Ridge at an elevation of 8,700 feet in the Manti-La Sal National Forest. The route ends about 48 miles later at the junction of SR-211. Allow three to four hours driving time.

Road Conditions: Parts of this Backway are accessible for passenger vehicles during dry weather, but the majority of the route requires high clearance vehicles. The Elk Ridge Road has a single lane, dirt surface. During the winter and after heavy rains it is impassable.

Scenery and Attractions: This drive offers scenic panoramas of Canyonlands National Park, Dark Canyon Wilderness, Arch, Allen and Hammond Canyons, the Henry and La Sal Mountains, and Monument Valley. Amidst forests of pinyon, juniper, pine and aspen are several BLM and National Forest recreation trails. One popular trail leads into Dark Canyon Wilderness. You will see several ponderosa pine trees with peeled bark along the route – the bark was eaten as food in the late 1800s by starving Native Americans.

41 ABAJO LOOP

Traveling This Backway: The Abajo Loop travels west from Monticello on Forest Road (FR) 105 to the junction with FR 079 then south through North Canyon to North Creek Pass where it turns northwest below Horsehead Peak and then southwest as it travels through the pine, fir, and aspen forest. The highest elevation reached along the roadway is 10,300 feet. The Backway ends in the community of Blanding, just over 35 miles from the beginning . Allow two hours travel time.

Road Conditions: High clearance vehicles are recommended for this Backway. Some portions are accessible in a passenger vehicle, but only during dry weather. The road has a single lane, and is either gravel or dirt. During winter and after heavy rains it is impassable.

Scenery and Attractions: The tranquil Abajo Loop takes visitors from the heat of the red rock desert floor into the heart of the Abajo Mountains. The Abajo, also known as the Blue Mountains, offer year-round recreation including opportunities to climb, drive or hike to summits over 11,000 feet. In addition to mountain recreation, the road offers impressive panoramas of Canyonlands National Park and surrounding mountain ranges in the Four Corners Region.

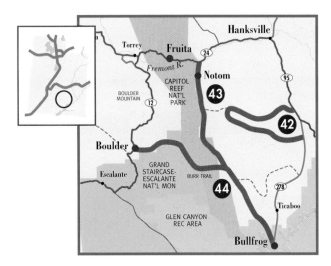

44 BURR TRAIL

Traveling This Backway: The Burr Trail is located between SR-12 at Boulder and SR-276 near Bullfrog Marina on Lake Powell. In between, it crosses the Waterpocket Fold of Capitol Reef National Park. The route is about 70 miles long and requires approximately 4 and one-half hours to travel.

Road Conditions: The Backway is both a paved and dirt road. The road from Boulder through Grand Staircase-Escalante National Monument to the boundary of Capitol Reef National Park is paved. The road through the Park to Bullfrog is primarily graded dirt with sections of improved gravel as well as portions of unmaintained dirt road. The Burr Trail has some steep grades in places and the road is frequently washboarded. During dry weather, severe dust conditions may be encountered. This Backway may be traveled in a passenger car during good weather, but high clearance or four-wheel drive vehicles may be necessary during some times of the year. Caution should be taken in inclement weather as clay soils make it easy to get stuck when wet.

Scenery and Attractions: This Backway offers an unparalleled sightseeing experience. The Burr Trail provides access to Grand Staircase-Escalante National Monument and Capitol Reef National Park while crossing miles of spectacular canyon country. The road climbs through stretches of red and yellow slickrock to vantage points where the Henry Mountains and much of southeastern Utah are in view. On portions of the route the Backway cuts through deep cool canyons where red sandstone walls tower 800 feet on either side. Some of the trail's most popular and challenging features are the switchbacks winding through the Waterpocket Fold portion of Capitol Reef National Park.

42 BULL CREEK PASS ROAD

Traveling This Backway: This Backway is accessed from SR-95 approximately 20 miles south of Hanksville. It runs west to McMillan Springs through Steven Narrows and loops east to SR-276, five miles south of SR-95. The route climbs from the desert floor to 10,500 feet at Bull Creek Pass passing through BLM public land. The road requires six to seven hours driving time and is 68 miles long, and is often impassable through June due to snow drifts.

Road Conditions: Bull Creek Pass Road has a single lane, dirt surface. Maintenance is infrequent. There are several rough places and steep grades. During the winter and after heavy rains it is impassable. High clearance vehicles are required and four-wheel drive vehicles are recommended to travel this Backway.

Scenery and Attractions: The route crosses BLM's Henry Mountains, the last range to be explored and named in the continental United States. This Backway provides unique vistas into the heart of the Colorado Plateau and often a glimpse of a free-roaming Buffalo herd. Beautiful canyons and erosional forms are plentiful. Other scenery ranges from colorful red cliffs, multi-hued hills and stark badlands at the lower elevations to mountains, forested and lush, grassy slopes higher up.

43 NOTOM ROAD

Traveling This Backway: Notom Road leads from SR-24 at the eastern boundary of Capitol Reef National Park to the junction of Burr Trail Road in the southern section of the park. This Backway is approximately 29 miles. Plan for one to two hours of driving time one-way, depending on the number of stops.

Road Conditions: This is a high grade dirt road, impassable during inclement weather. High clearance vehicles are recommended year-round.

Scenery and Attractions: Along its entire length the Notom Road parallels the Waterpocket Fold. This Backway provides an excellent opportunity to appreciate the magnitude of this colorful and desolate rock spine. East of the Backway, views of the Henry Mountains appear above softly rolling buttes of Mancos shale.

Frank Jensen

45 HOLE IN THE ROCK

Traveling This Backway: Traversing part of Grand-Staircase Escalante National Monument, this Backway begins five miles east of Escalante on SR-12 and leads to Hole-in-the-Rock at Lake Powell. This Scenic Backway generally parallels the route traveled in 1879 and 1880 by the Hole-in-the-Rock expedition of Mormon pioneers, who traveled from Escalante to the Colorado River. The road is 57 miles one way. Actual one way driving time is approximately four hours, however, round-trip, with exploration and photo stops, this Backway should be considered an all-day outing.

Road Conditions: The route runs between the Straight Cliffs of Fifty Mile Mountain and the canyons of the Escalante River. Its surface is gravel and graded dirt. Most of the road is suitable for passenger cars, but the last seven miles to Hole-in-the-Rock require a high-clearance four-wheel drive vehicle.

Scenery and Attractions: Attractions on this Backway include Dance Hall Rock, Soda Cabin and Devils Garden. The Straight Cliffs escarpment is in view the entire length of the route. At this road's end lies Hole-in-the-Rock, a slot in the wall of Glen Canyon through which Mormon Pioneers lowered their wagons to the river below. From Hole-in-the-Rock, the vista of Lake Powell is exceptional.

46 SMOKY MOUNTAIN ROAD

Traveling This Backway: Crossing the rugged landscape of the Kaiparowits Plateau, this road also traverses the Grand Staircase-Escalante National Monument, running north from the town of Big Water and arriving at Escalante and Highway 12. The Backway is 78 miles long and driving time is five hours. This is a lightly traveled road and water should be carried in case of emergency.

Road Conditions: Although the Smoky Mountain Road is graded dirt and gravel, it is recommended only for high-clearance or four-wheel drive vehicles. The Warm Creek badlands and Kelly Grade portions are impassable when wet and should not be attempted. The whole road can be very dusty during dry weather and sections are always rough and rutted.

Scenery and Attractions: After climbing five miles of switchbacks on the 1,200-foot face of Smoky Mountain via the Kelly Grade, the rocky sprawl of the Kaiparowits Plateau dominates the scenery of the route. Prior to reaching the plateau, the Warm Creek badlands in Glen Canyon Recreational Area may be remembered as settings in *The Greatest Story Every Told* and *Planet of the Apes*. This Backway offers spectacular views of Lake Powell, Navajo Mountain, Fifty Mile Mountain and further on, Bryce Canyon, the Table Cliffs and Boulder Mountain.

47 POSEY LAKE ROAD

Traveling This Backway: This Backway is 40 miles long. It begins in Escalante on Forest Road 153 and travels north through the Dixie National Forest ending at the town of Bicknell. The recommended travel time is a little over an hour.

Road Conditions: The road is primarily single lane dirt with some gravel surface. There are plenty of turnouts. The Backway is closed during winter months.

Scenery and Attractions: In the southern portion of this route, the Antone Ridge, a large anticline with exposed red rock formations, parallels the road. Large ponderosa pines grow from cracks in the rock. Thirteen miles from Escalante, you will come to a fork in the road. The right fork goes to Hells Backbone and the left fork, which is the Backway route, goes to Posey Lake and Bicknell. Posey Lake offers camping, fishing and trail access to other mountain lakes. From Posey Lake, the road climbs to the top of a plateau. Large open meadows mixed with dense stands of spruce and fir dominate the landscape. Sunrises and sunsets from the plateau are magnificent.

48 GRIFFIN TOP ROAD

Traveling This Backway: The Griffin Top Road begins at Posey Lake, in the Dixie National Forest, (see Posey Lake Road Backway) and curves southwest to the remains of the Widtsoe settlement. The route is 32 miles long and requires approximately one hour.

Road Conditions: This is a narrow, single lane dirt road with turnouts. The surface is partially gravel and may be driven by passenger vehicles. The Backway is closed in the winter.

Scenery and Attractions: From Posey Lake in its forest setting, this road continues through stands of spruce and fir. The Backway ascends to a plateau top filled with forests and meadows. Four and a half miles above the lake, the route takes a sharp turn south. This section of the plateau is excellent for wildlife viewing. As the road begins to descend, western views open across John's Valley to Mount Dutton. At the route's end you'll come to the old town of Widtsoe, which was once a farming and ranching community, until cold weather and drought drove people from the area.

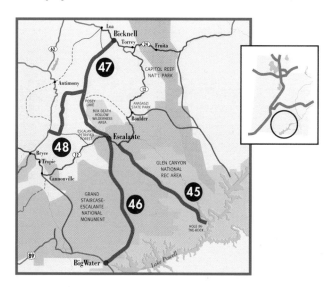

49 COTTONWOOD CANYON ROAD

Traveling This Backway: This colorful Backway traverses the Grand Staircase-Escalante National Monument from US-89 east of BLM's Paria Ranger Station to Cannonville on SR-12. The road is 46 miles long and requires approximately three hours driving time.

Road Conditions: The majority of this road is graded dirt. Long dry periods cause severe washboard conditions and make roads very dusty. When wet, the portion of the road south of Kodachrome Basin State Park is impassable to most vehicles. The entire route is often impassable during extremely wet weather.

Scenery and Attractions: Providing access between Bryce Canyon National Park and Glen Canyon National Recreation Area (Lake Powell), this road receives heavy use during summer. The route features strangely eroded rock forms in Cottonwood Canyon and Kodachrome Basin State Park. A popular feature is BLM's Grosvenor Arch, a soaring pastel buttress located about ten miles east of the Kodachrome Basin turn-off. In Cottonwood Canyon, the sandstone colors are particularly striking. The Paria River and the rugged up thrust of the Cockscomb formation are also prominent features of this journey.

50 JOHNSON CANYON/ALTON AMPHITHEATER

Traveling This Backway: This 32-mile excursion through the Grand Staircase of Vermillion, White and Pink Cliffs begins on US-89, nine miles east of Kanab. The Backway loops back to US-89 at Glendale, 26 miles north of Kanab. Driving time is two hours. An alternate spur on the Backway travels north to Alton with closer views of the Pink Cliffs. This spur connects to US-89 nine miles north of Glendale.

Road Conditions: The first 15 miles of the Backway through Johnson Canyon are paved. The remainder of the road is maintained gravel suitable for year-round travel by passenger cars. The gravel portions of the Backway may impassable after heavy snow or rainstorms.

Scenery and Attractions: Settled as early as 1871, the working ranches of Johnson Canyon retain their historical heritage. Six miles into the Backway, a film set from TV's *Gunsmoke* adds to the western flavor. Much of this red rock setting is on private land, but the paved rod offers excellent windshield and roadside sightseeing. Views of the White Cliff with a Pink Cliff backdrop begin in upper Johnson Valley. The pavement ends at the top of the White Cliffs. From here, the Backway turns west to highlight the pink cliffs of the Alton Amphitheater and some extinct volcano cones in the vicinity of Bald Knoll. An eastern fork of the road (not part of the Backway) continues for 38 miles beneath the Pink Cliffs of Bryce Canyon Amphitheater to Cannonville on SR-12.

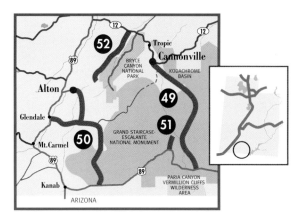

51 PARIA RIVER VALLEY

Traveling This Backway: In the Paria River Valley of the Grand Staircase-Escalante National Monument, a northward spur of US-89 located 40 miles east of Kanab provides access to this short, five mile Backway. The Backway leads to western film locations and the ghost town of Pahreah. Visitors should plan to spend an hour exploring the area.

Road Conditions: This dirt road is graded and regularly maintained. Passenger car travel is not recommended after rain storms.

Scenery and Attractions: The scenery along this route has appeared in some of the most colorful westerns ever filmed. The ghost town of Old Pahreah is nestled in a colorful rock basin. Pahreah was named for a Paiute Indian word meaning "Muddy Water." A Mormon farming community in the late 1860s and early 1870s, Pahreah lost most of its residents following severe flooding in the mid 1880s. All that remains of Pahreah today are ruins and a small cemetery. Nearby, a pioneer town movie set, built in 1963 for the film *Sergeants Three*, invites exploration.

52 EAST FORK OF THE SEVIER

Traveling This Backway: This Backway departs from SR-12, 14 miles east of its junction with US-89, running through the Dixie National Forest to terminate at the forest's southern border. The road is 60 miles long and travel time is approximately one and one-half hours.

Road Conditions: This road is double lane gravel for nearly half its length. From there it is a single lane gravel with turnouts. The entire Backway is suitable for passenger cars. This route should be traveled in fair weather only.

Scenery and Attractions: The Backway is located in a broad valley scattered with ponderosa pine. Panoramic views open in all directions. Red rock formations and other geologic features are visible along the road. Mid-route is Tropic Reservoir, providing fishing, boating and camping. This route follows the east fork of the Sevier River, which meanders near the road. At the Backway's end, the Podunk Guard Station, built in 1928, exhibits a uniquely constructed pyramidal roof, the only one of its type used in the region.

Frank Jensen

PONDEROSA / CORAL PINK SAND DUNES

Traveling This Backway: Embarking from US-89 about seven miles north of Kanab, this route travels south to Coral Pink Sand Dunes State Park. The Backway is 12 miles long, one way, and requires 30 minutes driving time.

Road Conditions: Most of this road is gravel surfaced. However, a short portion is paved. The road is accessible year-round for passenger vehicles.

Scenery and Attractions: From US-89, the Backway climbs toward Coral Pink Sand Dunes State Park with views to the east of the White Cliffs and Pink Cliffs of Bryce Canyon National Park. A ponderosa pine forest parallels the edge of the Coral Pink Sand Dunes. The fine pink sand of the dunes is the product of erosion of the surrounding cliffs and ridges. Contrasting their unique colors, the dunes are dotted with ponderosa pines and wildflowers.

SMITHSONIAN BUTTE

Traveling This Backway: This Backway is accessed from SR-59, eight miles west of Hildale and runs north to the Rockville Bridge before joining SR-9 in Rockville. It is nine miles long each way, and you should plan on one hour travel time including stops.

Road Conditions: With the exception of a one-mile paved portion, this is a double lane graded dirt road. It is regularly maintained and can be safely driven in a normal passenger car. The Backway has a one-half mile section with steep grade. The road is open year-round but travel is not recommended during inclement weather.

Scenery and Attractions: The major features of this Backway are the BLM's Canaan Mountain and Smithsonian Butte landmarks and an outside-the-park panorama of Zion National Park featuring the East and West Temples and North Guardian Angel. Spectacular views are offered of the Virgin River Valley, Eagle Crags and the 2,000-foot headwall at The Pines. Because views change with vehicle direction, it is recommended that this route be driven in both directions.

KOLOB RESERVOIR ROAD

Traveling This Backway: This Backway covers the area from SR-9 at Virgin, north to SR-14 six miles east of Cedar City. The route is approximately 45 miles long. With photo stops, this Backway takes about two hours to travel.

Road Conditions: Backway conditions range from paved and gravel to graded dirt. The road is suitable for passenger cars. Parts of the route on the descending side are steep and impassable during extremely wet conditions. The road is closed during winter months.

Scenery and Attraction: This route takes visitors through grassy meadows to ascend the red and white sandstone ledges of Zion National Park. It provides a view of the west side of the park not available in any other location. Kolob Reservoir at 8,000 feet provides fishing and summer recreation. From the top of Kolob Terrace, the red walled mesas of the Kolob Canyons section of Zion National Park are prominent. As the Backway nears its end, the northern portions of the drive are thickly forested.

DRY LAKES / SUMMIT CANYON

Traveling This Backway: This route begins just north of the town of Summit on old US-91. Traveling southeast through private land and the Dixie National Forest, the Backway ends at SR-143 eight miles south of Parowan. The total distance of this drive is approximately 19 miles. Travel time is one hour.

Road Conditions: This is an improved road with gravel on some sections. It is narrow and steep in areas, but may be traveled in a passenger car with care. Travel is not recommended in wet weather. The Backway is closed during winter months.

Scenery and Attractions: The first portion of this road climbs in elevation while offering panoramic views into Cedar Canyon, Summit Canyon and the "checkerboard" fields of the Summit-Parowan Valley. The midpoint of the drive is Sugarloaf Mountain at about 9,000 feet. From here the road descends, crossing several small streams and meadows. This Backway also provides sweeping, photo-worthy views of Ashdown Gorge and Cedar Breaks National Monument.

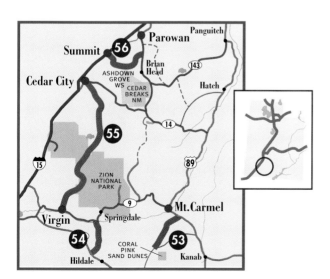

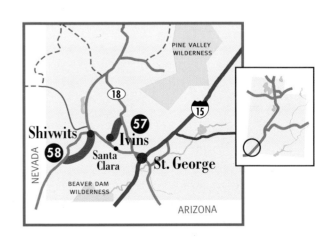

58 MOJAVE DESERT/JOSHUA TREE ROAD

Traveling This Backway: Two miles north of the Utah/Arizona border, this Backway begins at the Joshua Tree National Landmark junction on old US-91. The road leads northeast to rejoin old US-91 approximately two miles south of Shivwits. Plan one to two hours to travel this 16-mile loop with stops.

Road Conditions: The Backway is a maintained gravel and dirt road. It is suitable for passenger cars most of the year. The route is never closed, but does have truck traffic from a local mining company. It is recommended that drivers travel the road at 15 to 20 miles per hour.

Scenery and Attractions: This route accesses BLM's Joshua Tree National Landmark. It is the furthest north that Joshua Trees grow. From this area, the Backway features Mojave Desert landscapes and stunning wildflowers in season. Following Bulldog Canyon, the road parallels the wilderness boundary of the Beaver Dam Mountains. After skirting the base of Jarvis Peak to Wittwer Canyon, the Backway crosses the Shivwits Indian Reservation for three miles before reaching its terminus.

Large Photo: An ancient pinyon kisses the sky, somewhere in Utah — Mel Lewis

57 SNOW CANYON ROAD

Traveling This Backway: This Backway begins in the town of Ivins and travels north through Snow Canyon State Park (fee area) before joining SR-18. The road is approximately seven miles long. Even with photo stops and brief exploration, this route takes less than an hour to travel.

Road Conditions: The Snow Canyon Road is entirely paved and open year-round.

Scenery and Attractions: The Backway highlights three-mile long Snow Canyon. This colorful area features sculptured sandstone cliffs, unusual volcanic cinder cones and lava tubes, and sand dunes. Native American rock art may be viewed via short hikes. The State Park is open year-round and has a campground and picnic area.

FOR MORE INFORMATION ON SCENIC BYWAYS AND BACKWAYS CONTACT ANY OF THESE COOPERATING AGENCIES:

UTAH STATE

Utah Travel Council
300 North State Street, SLC, UT 84114-1369
801-538-1030, 800-200-1160, www.utah.com

Utah State Parks and Recreation
1594 West North Temple, Suite 116
PO Box 146001 , SLC, UT 84114-6001
801-538-7220, www.stateparks.utah.gov

Utah State Parks Northwest Region Office
1084 North Redwood Road, SLC, UT 84116-1555
801-533-5127

Utah State Parks Northeast Region Office
S.R. 319, 777 West Box 3, Heber, UT 84032
435-649-9109

Utah State Parks Southwest Region Office
585 North Main, Cedar City, UT 84720
435-586-4497

Utah State Parks Southeast Region Office
1165 S. Highway 191, Suite 7, Moab, UT 84532-3062
435-259-3750

BUREAU OF LAND MANAGEMENT

Bureau of Land Management Utah State Office
324 South State Street, Suite 301
P.O. Box 45155, Salt Lake City, UT 84145-0155
(801) 539-4001, www.ut.blm.gov

Cedar City BLM District Office
176 East D.L. Sargent Drive, Cedar City, UT 84720
(435) 586-2401, www.ut.blm.gov/cedarcity-fo

Kanab BLM Field Office
318 North 100 East, Kanab, UT 84741
(435) 644-4600, www.ut.blm.gov/kanab-fo

**Grand Staircase-Escalante National Monument
Kanab BLM Headquarters**
180 West 300 North, Kanab, UT 84741
(435) 644-4300, www.ut.blm.gov/monument

**Grand Staircase-Escalante National Monument
Escalante BLM Interagency Office & Visitor Center**
P.O. Box 225, (755 W. Main Street), Escalante, UT 84726
Office (435) 826-5600, Visitor Center (435) 826-5499
www.ut.blm.gov/monument

**Grand Staircase-Escalante National Monument
Cannonville BLM Visitor Center**
10 Center Street, P.O. Box 189961, Cannonville, UT 84718
Office: (435) 679-8980, Visitor Center (435) 679-8981
www.ut.blm.gov/monurnent

St. George BLM Field Office
345 East Riverside Drive, St. George, UT 84790
(435) 688-3200, www.ut.blm.gov/stgeorge-fo/sgfonews.html

Richfield BLM Field Office
150 East 900 North, Richfield, UT 84701
(435) 896-1500

Henry Mountain BLM Field Station
P.O. Box 99, Hanksville, UT 84734
(435) 542-3461

Fillmore BLM Field Office
35 East 500 North, Fillmore, UT 84631
(435) 743-3100

Moab BLM Field Office
82 East Dogwood, Moab, UT 84532
(435) 259-6111, www.blm.gov/utah/moab

Price BLM Field Office
125 South 600 West, Price, UT 84501
(435) 636-3600, www.blm.gov/utah/price

Monticello BLM field Office
435 North Main Street, P.O. Box 7, Monticello, UT 84535
(435) 587-1500, www.blm.gov/utah/monticello

Vernal BLM Field Office
170 South 500 East, Vernal, UT 84078
(435) 781-4400, www.blm.gov/utah/vernal

Salt Lake City BLM Field Office
2370 South 2300 West, Salt Lake City, UT 84119
(435) 977-4300, www.ut.blm.gov/saltlake-fo

NATIONAL PARK SERVICE

Arches National Park
PO Box 907, Moab, UT 84532
435-259-8161, www.nps.gov/arch

Bryce Canyon National Park
Bryce Canyon, UT 84717
435-834-5322, www.nps.gov/brca

Canyonlands National Park
Moab, UT 84532
435-259-7164, www.nps.gov/cany

Capitol Reef National Park
HC-70, Box 15, Torrey, UT 84775
435-425-3791, www.nps.gov/care

Cedar Breaks National Monument
2390 W Hwy 56, #11, Cedar City, UT 84720
435-586-9451, www.nps.gov/cebr

Dinosaur National Monument
Quarry Visitor Center
PO Box 128, Jensen, UT 84035
435-789-2115, www.nps.gov/dino

Hovenweep National Monument
McElmo Rt, Cortez, CO 81312
970-749-0510, www.nps.gov/hove

Natural Bridges National Monument
Box 1, Lake Powell, UT 84533
435-692-1234, www.nps.gov/nabr

Zion National Park
PO Box 1099, Springdale, UT 84767
435-772-3256, www.nps.gov/zion

UNITED STATES FOREST SERVICE

Ashley National Forest
355 North Vernal Ave, Vernal, UT 84078
435-789-1181, www.fs.fed.us/r4/ashley

Flaming Gorge National Recreation Area
Junction Hwy 43 and 44, PO Box 279, Manila, UT 84046
435-789-1181

Dixie National Forest Cedar City Ranger District
1789 North Wedgewood Drive, Cedar City, UT 84720
435-865-3200, www.fs.fed.us/dxnf

Fishlake National Forest
115 East 900 North, Richfield, Utah 84701
435-896-9233 , www.fs.fed.us/r4/fishlake

Uinta National Forest
88 West 100 North, PO Box 1428, Provo, Utah 84601
801-342-5100, www.fs.fed.us/r4/uinta

Wasatch-Cache National Forest
8236 Federal Bldg, 125 S State St., SLC, UT 84138
801-524-3900, www.fs.fed.us/wcnf

Manti-La Sal National Forest
599 West Price River Drive, Price, UT 84501
435-637-2817, www.fs.fed.us/r4/mantilasal

TREAD LIGHTLY! PLEDGE:

- TRAVEL and RECREATE with minimum impact
- RESPECT the environment and the rights of others
- EDUCATE yourself, PLAN and PREPARE before you go
- ALLOW for future use of the outdoors,
  LEAVE it better than you found it
- DISCOVER the rewards of responsible recreation

Canyon Country MINIMUM IMPACT PRACTICES – Bureau of Land Management

Each year, millions of visitors enjoy Canyon Country. The impact of so much use is threatening the area's biological and cultural resources. You can help protect this fragile and beautiful land by following these five minimum-impact practices.

TREAD LIGHTLY when Traveling – LEAVE NO TRACE when Camping

Drive and ride only on roads and trails where such travel is allowed: hike only on established trails, on rock, or in washes. Camp at designated sites or, where allowed, at previously-used sites. Avoid placing tents on top of vegetation and use a camp stove instead of making a campfire. Unless signs indicate otherwise, leave gates open or closed as you find them.

Help Keep Canyon Country Clean

Pack out your trash and recycle it, clean up after less thoughtful visitors, and dispose of human waste properly.

Protect and Conserve Desert Water Sources

Water is scare in the desert. Camp at least 300 feet from isolated water sources to allow for wildlife access. Where possible, carry your own drinking water. Leave potholes undisturbed and wash well away from pools and springs.

Allow Space for wildlife

When encountering wildlife, maintain your distance and remain quiet. Teach children not to chase or pick up animals. Keep pets under control.

Leave Historic Sites, Native American Rock Art, Ruins and Artifacts Untouched for the Future

Admire rock art from a distance and never touch it. Stay out of ruins, leave artifacts in place, and report violations.

"Utah! SCENIC Byways and Backways" is a publication of the Utah Travel Council, U.S. Bureau of Land Management, U.S. Forest Service, Utah Department of Transportation, Utah Travel Regions, Association of Governments, Utah State Parks and Recreation, National Park Service and Federal Highway Administration.
© 2002 All Rights Reserved.